Fisher Press

WAR DIARY

Hugh Everard Dormer was born in 1919, the second son of Kenelm Dormer and Josephine Toohey. He was a great-grandson on his father's side of Kenelm Digby, the nineteenth-century writer on chivalry and the spirit of Christendom. The Dormers are one of Britain's most distinguished recusant families. Hugh Dormer was educated at Ampleforth, where he was Head Monitor, and at Christchurch, Oxford where he read history. His university career was interrupted by the outbreak of the Second World War.

Like his father he was commissioned in the Irish Guards. He served with the 2nd Armoured Battalion in Britain until October 1942. An inter-service liaison scheme provided him with a trip on a destroyer, which saw action in the Channel against an armed German merchant cruiser, and gave him a glimpse of the coast of German-occupied France. Inspired by this, and with a desire for action, he volunteered for clandestine work in France with the Special Operations Executive (SOE).

SOE was formed in July 1940 to coordinate subversion and sabotage against the enemy overseas. Its dangerous missions were to show the French that they were not alone, and hence foster a revival of their will to resist the Germans, which had been broken by the Franco-German armistice of the summer of 1940, and the creation of the Vichy Government; and to sap German confidence by acts of economic sabotage.

Hugh Dormer was twice parachuted into France as leader of raiding parties to damage a shale oil refinery near Autun, which was making fuel for the German armoured divisions in Russia and North Africa. The first mission failed; the second was successful. On his return to Britain he was awarded the DSO. He was offered an enhanced role working with SOE in Western France, but, after much heart-searching, returned to his Regiment in January 1944.

He was a troop leader of No 2 Tank Squadron of the Armoured Battalion in the D day landings, and took part in the armoured attack east of Caen in the third week of July. On 1 August 1944 he was killed in an action to take high ground in the Bocage near St. Martin des Besaces. As a young man he wrote poetry and reflective essays of considerable insight. The *War Diary* covers the events of a little over a year; it is partly derived from his notebooks and partly from the military reports he prepared on returning to Britain.

A NOTE WRITTEN BY HUGH DORMER IN HIS DIARY IN JULY 1943

Again and again one gets that moment of intuition, that sudden vision of how the old world is falling into chaos around us. Ideas and principles that have never yet been challenged in the centuries are questioned for the first time by scientific unbelievers; the traditions of the army, the security of classes and the respect of man for his superiors, the values of religion, the sacredness of the family itself are all violated and derided. While everything that he has been brought up to believe in falls around him, man feels that he must strike out alone into the new future and seek for himself the unprecedented pattern of the adventure of his own life. There is no security or faith left anywhere save in the tower of his own mind, while the darkening storm rages outside louder and louder with ever increasing violence. All, all is being swept into ruin and dissolution as never before; the very pillars of the West are falling.

HUGH DORMER DSO

WAR DIARY

with a Foreword by
Cardinal Basil Hume OSB

and a Preface by
Abbot Patrick Barry OSB

With maps, a military sketch plan, a line drawing by John
Dormer, his artist brother, and Hugh Dormer's account of a
naval action against a German convoy in the English
Channel not previously published

Fisher Press

Published by Fisher Press, Post Office Box 41,
Sevenoaks, Kent, TN15 6YN, England

Hugh Dormer's *Diary* was first published in 1947
First published as a Fisher paperback 1994
Reprinted with new Foreword & Preface 1998
Copyright in the text © John Dormer
Copyright in the Foreword © Cardinal Basil Hume OSB
Copyright in the Preface © Abbot Patrick Barry OSB

British Library Cataloguing in Publication Data.
A catalogue record for this book is available from
The British Library

ISBN 1 874037 11 6

Typesetting Consultant: Grand Designs, London
Printed by Antony Rowe Ltd., Wiltshire
Cover: Sol Communications Ltd., London

FOREWORD

I am delighted that Abbot Patrick Barry has provided a Preface to this new printing of Fisher Press' edition of Hugh Dormer's *War Diary*. He was nearer to being a contemporary of Hugh at Ampleforth than I, and was closely involved with the family in editing the first edition of the diaries in 1947.

It was Abbot Patrick Barry who has particularly sought to ensure that the importance and significance of Hugh Dormer's short life is not forgotten. In his Preface he vividly recalls the political and social ills which those of Hugh Dormer's generation had to face when growing up, and shows how his faith enabled him to see things more clearly than many others of his generation. Although the challenges faced by the young of today are not the same as those which had to be confronted when Hugh Dormer was coming into manhood, yet the insight and clarity of vision which he displays in his diaries make him a hero who has much to teach us today.

Basil Hume OSB
Archbishop of Westminster

DEDICATION OF THIS EDITION

This edition has only been made possible through the kindness and friendship of Kathleen and John Dormer. It is dedicated to them both. They not only gave permission to republish the *Diary*, but also allowed us to include in this edition Hugh Dormer's account of the naval action which, as the *Diary* makes clear, encouraged him to take on the work for the Special Operations Executive. This part of the *Diary* has not previously been published. John Dormer, the artist brother of Hugh Dormer, has also allowed us to use his line drawing of mountains at the end of the Diary.

John and Hugh Dormer spent part of their childhood in sight of Mount Kenya. Mountains have been a recurrent theme in John Dormer's work as an artist; as the *Diary* reveals they were also destined to play an important part in Hugh Dormer's escape following his wartime work in France. They continue to have a special spiritual significance for the link between the two brothers.

ACKNOWLEDGEMENTS

We are grateful to the Imperial War Museum, London for permission to reproduce on the cover a detail of William Dring's pastel, A Stick of Paratroopers jumping at Ringway, 1945; and to John Dormer, for permission to reproduce the photograph of Hugh Dormer in the vignette.

Contents

PREFACE

BY ABBOT PATRICK BARRY OSB

The world of the thirties, in which Hugh Dromer grew up, was far removed from the world of today. There is this likeness, however, that at both times there was much confusion about values and aims, and little to inspire the young with new visions to transform sordid political programmes.

While Hugh was a boy at school at Ampleforth unemployment was a running sore in our society and no-one knew what to do about it. Even in that remote Yorkshire countryside there was a camp for the unemployed within sight of the school. The rows of huts looking down on the valley were a grim icon of the camps that would soon spread all over Europe—the army camps, the camps for prisoners of war, the concentration camps, the camps for displaced persons. It looked forward to all that evil and it looked back to the great depression which was a living memory threatening our peace of mind. Mobs were feared and sometime fearsome. Children went barefoot in the streets of Liverpool, and the faces of the Jarrow marchers haunted the pictures in the press and on the newsreels in the cinemas. Edward, the Prince of Wales, on a visit to the settled horrors of depressed South Wales hit the headlines with the impatient royal cry "Something must be done." But it remained a cry of agony rather than an effective summons to action. No-one seemed to know what to do.

Except, of course, the dictators. They always knew exactly what to do; it was the Age of the Dictators. Hitler was growing to power in the early thirties, and the clever commentators laughed at him, reassuring us all that he would come to nothing; but after 1933 all that changed. His power grew and grew. We read of the brutal attack on the Jews on *Kristallnacht* and the first Jewish refugees came to live in our village. Hitler had come to power when everyone was looking the other way—especially the United

States, which was passively locked in the dream of isolationism guaranteed by law, until the dream was shattered by Japan in 1941. And anyway Hitler was joining the forward-looking club that was bestriding the world—the club of the dictators. Mussolini had made the trains run on time and drained the Pontine marshes, and proclaimed the new Roman Empire as he colonised North Africa. *Mare nostrum*—our own private sea—is what he called the Mediterranean. Everyone who liked punctuality and good drainage and colonialism had something good to say of Mussolini in those days, while too many Catholics thought him Catholic. The Civil War ravaged Spain and infected France and Britain with the deep divisions of opposing ideologies. Franco emerged as a dictator with Spain in an iron grip. Salazar had a grip on Portugal. Stalin had a grip on Russia. No-one really had a grip on Britain, but our left-leaning intelligentsia gazed in admiring ecstasy on Stalin as they painted idealised pictures of the delights of the Soviet regime. A series of books came out which we read in the school library, called rather grandly "Makers of the Modern Age." Each of the dictators had a volume to himself, but there was no grand champion of democracy. Democracy did not seem to be working; unemployent and poverty told us that. Hitler had abolished unemployment and the pink brigade of intellectuals told us that Stalin had abolished poverty. No-one seemed to have a counter-vision. To many the future seemed to lie with the dictators.

The moderates looked ever hopefully to the League of Nations, but it did nothing to stop the dictators, except noble gestures which were both pathetic and powerless. In Britain, the left wingers joined the Communist Party, and the extreme right went fascist under Mosley. One Old Boy of the School, when Hugh Dormer was in the Sixth Form, came in a black shirt to our debating society seeking converts to fascism. He was faced by another Old Boy in a different coloured shirt for an evening of the typical political wrangling which ended in nothing but exhausted confusion. The confusion and erosion of values went deeper than we thought at the time. The sordid age of double-talk and double-think was quietly taking root around the left wing dons and the secret agents growing up at Cambridge. In the Oxford Union debating society the other young hopefuls of the nation made world news by an overwhelming vote that they would not fight for king and country.

This was the confusion in which Hugh grew to manhood. He took a lively and intelligent part in all the heart-searching to which it led while he was at school and at university. But he wasn't torn apart by it and he did not lose his way. That was the miracle with him and many others as the thirties moved towards their dreadful conclusions. For those who knew him as he grew up he was a delightful companion and friend with a depth and stability of character that drew others to look to him for a lead. He had a lively sense of humour and a strong literary instinct. He began writing quite seriously as a small boy in the lowest form in the school. It was not particular isolated gifts that were impressive in him, but a roundness and depth of personality in which his mind-set or rather soul-set was radically Catholic. Catholicism was not an addition to his other personal gifts; it was of the essence of his personality; it was what made him what he became. He had learnt from the tradition of his growing up, both in his family and his school, to value that wholeness of mind and heart and soul which had belonged to the Catholic tradition through the dark ages of negation and persecution. That wholeness stood him in good stead in the age of confusion which was the thirties. Nothing is reflected in his diaries so radiantly as this deep Catholicism. There was nothing inward looking or defensive about it. It was outward looking, unafraid and all-embracing; it remained undismayed even by the hideous battlefields of Europe.

He is typical of many others who strode out of the confusion and contradictions of the thirties to give everything, when they were faced with the obscenities of Nazism: for the salvation, not only of their country, but, as he saw it, of

Christian civilisation as well. His diaries are explicit about this. He and many of his generation had preserved an integrity, a wholeness that stood them—and all of us—in good stead at the time of crisis and horror. There was more of this wholeness among his contemporaries in the universities than anyone—least of all Hitler— could have expected from the wild uncertainties and conflicts of the times. We lurched through the decade in a welter of false values until we were faced with the shock of Munich and the first great capitulation and human sacrifice—the human sacrifice of the Czechs which was followed so inevitably by the rape of Poland, under the combined attack of the human predators of German Nazis and Russian Soviets. After that there was a great silence in Britain when everyone slowly recognised that they knew what was to come, and what they had to do about it. That was when the young in the mould of Hugh Dormer came into their own.

Hugh Dormer's *War Diary* is good reading, but it is not a great war story. Secret operations like his are discounted by the experts of today—in just the same way as much of the conduct of the war, whether rightly or wrongly, is dismissed by academics as incompetence. It may be that Hugh and his generation came from the confusion of the thirties into the muddle of the war. But what is of value is his personal, human, Catholic and self-giving perception of and dedication to what really matters—whether in war or peace. It is especially in the last part of the *War Diary* that all this is revealed with a sensitive eloquence that is rare and time-less. He had no illusions. He did not blind himself with mindless courage. He did not abandon thought for action. He knew what he was about:

There can be very little idealism about war at the time, but only a lot of dirt and fear and sickening ignominy. It is only in retrospect or in the romantic minds of those who have never witnessed the horrors of a battlefield that glory is seen. And yet, after my experience I know, what I originally surmised, that the only happy man is he who serves some ideal other than his own self-interest...There is so much in the world to appreciate and so much goodness in each individual human being to love that it would take an eternity to complete, and yet at the end of it all to die for God and one's country and one's fellow men would be the greatest blessing of all. (p. 117)

It was in the shadow of the invasion that he revealed himself most fully in the diaries that he wrote for his mother. He was strangely certain that he would be killed. He accepted that and faced everything—the past, the future, the fate of civilisation, the truth of Christianity, in deep conversations with Dom Julian Stonor (a monk of Downside who during the war served as chaplain to the Irish Guards).

Certain people like Julian Stonor are intended as beacons to the world, reminding men of the eternal existence of those high ideals which call men out against all reason and self-interest; and if there came a time when the race of such sentinels as he had died out or were fallen asleep, then humanity would sink into perpetual despair, seeing only its daily round of sordid suffering and dull monotony. (p. 116)

There are times when I feel the tide of happiness so mounting in my soul as though the flood-gates might burst and the frail body and its bonds break asunder. My soul is exhilarated like a bird that would sing forever till its lungs burst. No man ever went out to his fate more joyfully than I. (p. 124)

The motto of his family, which he quoted in his diaries with reverence and affection, had become a reality: from deep conviction, forged under the outward appearance of high-risk soldiering, he had made his own:
> Ciò che Dio Vuole io voglio.
> Whatever is God's will I also will for myself.

12 September 1998   Patrick Barry OSB

ORIGINAL DEDICATION

To my Mother

I am leaving you this book in case I never come back from this next journey and it is left to others to tell you.

When you read the pages, perhaps there is much that will shock you — like the photograph of your son in Paris in May 1943 looking like some hunted rat. But, as I have written at the end, I have thought on it a lot and understood each day more clearly what I am doing, as it is obviously the most important work of my life. If you do not like that photograph of your son, I can only remind you that we were playing at a desperate game walking on the knife-edge of danger to an extent you never really realized.

Ideals are romantic and noble at a distance and they shine through men like light through alabaster, but the mechanism of their practical accomplishment in the world is often sordid in the extreme. And therein lies the real test which will show whether those ideals are only illusions or whether they are founded on experience and understanding. Mine have lasted.

Christmas 1943

CHAPTER ONE

THE FIRST OPERATION IN FRANCE

FIRST LANDING IN OCCUPIED FRANCE

(Palm Sunday) April 18th, 1943

The evening sun was glowing on the brick walls of the kitchen garden and on the wild daffodils under the chestnut trees, as we made the final preparation for our journey that night. I sat in a chair outside and read Shakespeare's Henry V while the wind ruffled my hair. The tranquil atmosphere of an English country house provided a perfect prelude to our journey. The wind sang in my blood and this mellowness was of ancient times and of an ancient land, for which one would be proud to die.

After an early dinner we left for the aerodrome some few miles distant. Here in a hut we were helped into our parachute equipment which gave us finally the swollen air of some creature from Mars. Then in closed cars with blinds drawn we were driven out on to the tarmac runway of the airfield. Our Halifax was warming up and the Polish crew were having a final check-up of the controls. The sun was just setting behind the trees. A last handshake all round and the six of us clambered up into the fuselage.

The interior was spacious and, as we were not due over

the target area for some four hours, our parachute harness was not hooked up and we were able to walk about inside. We taxied up into the wind and took off, and for the next hour flew south over the coast. The Channel was silver as we droned steadily over it. As we approached the French coast we dived sharply down to tree-top level and crossed the line swerving to confuse the defences. Flak glowed up at us from either side a long way distant. As we flew low over the roads and fields and valleys — as clear as day in the brilliant moonlight — I watched every detail of the country with an extraordinary sense of detachment. So we flew on hour after hour into the heart of France as smoothly as though it were a peacetime pleasure cruise. During this time I had crawled forward past the pilot and down into the cockpit of the plane. And here I crouched looking over the shoulder of the navigator, who knelt with his maps around him by the windows. He had a red cushion under his knees and, Pole as he was, he might have been praying at a prie-dieu in some cathedral. Below us all the time flashed the ever changing panorama.

At midnight we saw in the distance two great fires, perhaps the work of earlier bombers. I crawled back into the fuselage where the others were drinking hot coffee and rum and eating sandwiches; then curling up in their sleeping-bags they went to sleep again on the floor. I sat and read some more of Henry V. About one o'clock we were approaching the target, so we were all made to sit down in our places and our static lines were hooked up. Then the doors over the hole were uncovered and sitting on the rim I gazed down at the fields and hedges five hundred feet below. I could see cars moving on the roads and cattle in the fields. Down in the cockpit the navigator must have been fever-ishly busy with his maps and wind-speed indicators, working out his last minute calculations, for it is a tricky business to drop men not bombs. As we came in over the target, the dis-patcher shouted, 'Action stations'. I swung my legs into the hole and waited tensed for the order to go. Next to me crouched D wrapped up like a round baby in all his clothes and looking rather frightened.

The dispatcher knelt on the side holding the package which he was going to throw out immediately before I was to jump. As the pilot presumably intended to circle again over the dropping point, the dispatcher gave me the cancellation signal with his hands and waved me to take my legs out of the hole again, which I did, presuming we should get the order 'Action stations' again before jumping. So for the next ten minutes I relaxed, sitting on the edge of the hole and looking down at the ground beneath trying to identify any landmarks. It was fortunate that I did so, for suddenly to my amazement I heard a loud bang and saw the container dropping away to earth, which was the first warning I had that we were going to drop. I knew that if I did not drop like lightning after that we should probably never see the container again, which in fact nearly happened. At the same time the thought flashed through my mind that perhaps they had changed the plan at the last minute, after seeing the ground, and that we were going to make two runs — dropping first the containers and packages and then us. However, I swung my legs into the hole and jumped instinctively. As I went through the hole I heard the dispatcher shout something; I was not sure whether it was 'Go' or 'Stop,' but in either case it was too late.

All then was peace and complete silence save for the soft rustle of silk above. It was with some relief that behind me I saw the rest of the stick floating against the moon. I drifted down over a hill past a wood and came to earth just short of a hedge. I saw next to mine John's parachute crumple and fall past me to the ground. He landed on his back and bruised his spine and I learnt later that higher up the hill L had a badly twisted ankle.

I don't think I shall ever forget the silence of those few moments after landing. I looked around and found myself alone in a small field about a hundred yards from the main road and some houses. The moonlight was flooding down and I could see for miles. The grass was drenched in dew. Of my companions not a sight or sound. It seemed impossible to realize that one was in the middle of France; the night was of peace; it had nothing to do with war.

I rolled up my parachute after some difficulty and exasperation as the string kept on breaking, and then I set off to look for my comrades. The hill was steep and I had to make a long detour to find gaps in the hedges. Sweating and thirsty I reached the top, but of any living thing not a sight. Down in the village the dogs were all barking furiously and every now and again I heard whistles as though the gendarmes were out. It was only later that I discovered a certain small bird which was responsible for the sound. I was sure that the others must have fallen in the village and either been caught or given the alarm, as they very nearly did.

I continued to tramp about the fields for the next two hours and stood on the skyline waving a luminous ball in all directions and, in fact, did everything possible to attract their attention. I still failed to see or hear anything of the rest of the party. So in disgust I entered a small wood and there stripping I dug a hole by the light of a shaded torch and buried my parachute and equipment. Then, putting on my mackintosh and hat, I returned to the search. At four o'clock I left the hill and went to the rendezvous, where the road ended at the edge of the village and a path went up between the woods. I lay down by the edge of a stream and drank greedily. The singing of the birds was continuous and I thought how much Julian Stonor[1] would have loved to be here. One experienced somehow — however incongruously — a great sense of freedom.

Soon after five-thirty I left the rendezvous and went and hid up in the woods near by and subsequently learnt that I must have just missed H who arrived at the rendezvous

[1] Fr Julian Stonor — a monk of Downside Abbey — was chaplain to the 2nd Battalion of Irish Guards in France before Dunkirk and in England until February 1944, when, for reasons of ill-health, he had to leave the battalion before the invasion.

about six a.m.

I sat up under the trees and waited till dawn. My chances of reaching Paris alone and extricating myself from my plight seemed remote. It was cold and I had only a bar of chocolate to eat and no other food. Soon after daybreak some peasants started to chop wood in the valley beneath and I could hear them talking in French. I still could not realize I had ever left England and they seemed most incongruous; only a few hours before I had been having dinner in the Midlands. I crawled into a patch of sunlight and began to get warm again. I ate some of the chocolate and of course my thirst returned.

At midday I pushed forward to the edge of the trees and looked down on the village and the sleeping fields. In all the valley there was nothing moving and no signs of men except smoke rising from one of the cottages. The whole countryside had the terrifying silence of a desert. All the men had been taken away to Germany and it was as though some giant had struck the houses and the fields and cast them into eternal sleep. I was the only thing that moved in that unmoving land.

I decided to go for a walk in the woods on the off-chance of finding somebody, and, after walking for about twenty minutes, as luck would have it I glimpsed a blue shirt through the leaves and heard some English being spoken, and so I found the rest of the party.

PREPARATION FOR THE ATTACK

It was then that I discovered that we had had two casualties on landing. I decided to send them to Paris immediately so as to give them as long a start as possible. I rearranged the pairs accordingly. I also learnt that B and D, on going down to draw some water in the morning, had by luck found the container, with its parachute, still lying in a field at ten a.m. Apparently they had made this discovery before the local inhabitants. They had dragged it into temporary cover in a hedge.

At three p.m. I set off with J and L to put them on the road to Paris as both of them had great difficulty even in hobbling.

We had a rather tiring afternoon walking round a field which a man was ploughing, and by the time we arrived at a stream where they intended to shave we discovered that both their wash-bags had fallen out on the way, which made the journey rather pointless. However, I arranged with them to leave my wash-bag under a bridge near by, as we had to pass the same way that night towards the target. I then left them and got back about eight p.m. feeling already rather tired.

At dusk, nine p.m., we moved down from the woods and set about dismantling the container. We carried the cells up the hill into a deserted pit that had a few trees in it. Here we opened the cells and packed the contents into the ruck-sacks and concealed everything else in the undergrowth and covered it all with leaves. We also discovered that the container had never been provided with any lights, which no doubt made it so difficult to find the night before.

When we had finished, it was found impossible to lift the rucksacks off the ground, so we had to repack them, discard-ing most of the chocolate, all the tea and sugar and about half the food. This made the weights just tolerable, though the charges stuck into one's back. I reckoned that each man must have carried about eighty lbs. all in one small ruck-sack. As it was raining hard all this time we put all our suits, boots and mackintoshes into three sandbags, and that con-stituted the fourth man's load. Thereby it was never possible to relieve each other on the journey. The blankets and the rest of the package we abandoned in the pit.

We set out walking about one a.m. because, although we were already exhausted, I decided that we could not afford to waste the rest of that night in the same place and I was anxious to cover at least a part of the journey before dawn. Furthermore, it would have been impossible to get any sleep in the rain and would only have made everything more miserable. Progress was slow as we were almost bent double under the rucksacks, and I should think we averaged about half a mile an hour and stopped for rests every twenty minutes. We followed a track for the first part down to the bridge where I left the wash-bag for L, but later on we had to move across the fields as the track would have led us through the village and, burdened down and quite incapable of running as we were, I was not going to take the risk of discovery. Instead we came out on the main road and had to walk along it for about ten minutes to find another gap in the hedge opposite. We had by now covered, I should think, two miles.

H and B said that they could go no farther with the loads and were completely out. I was only surprised myself they had been able to last as far as they did.

I left them just off the road and went on with D to find a resting place for the following day. Movement across country in that neighbourhood was extremely difficult as it was impossible to find or make a way through the hedges. Often we walked around all four sides of a field to find a gate and had to make considerable detours to get where we wanted. I finally discovered a suitable wood and we buried our two rucksacks there under some leaves. (The rucksacks we had to pass over the hedges and in this manner the straps of one broke. At the end I was too exhausted to carry anything farther and it was D who carried both loads over the last part of the fields.

We then went back and brought the other two up, and I hid the whole party in another small copse away from the charges. It was just getting light. Rain was still falling, and in any case we were soaked, so sleep was impossible.

We spent all day trying to dry our clothes and get warm and were hindered by frequent showers. The food from the very beginning was strictly rationed as I fully realized how vital a factor it was going to be. We got some muddy water from a ditch and made hot drinks on the cooker. We were not disturbed in this hide-out all day. In the afternoon I went out and reconnoitred the route for the night and also inspected the charges which seemed in good condition and fairly dry. We mended the rucksack with a strip of barbed wire. We moved off again that night at dusk, about nine-thirty.

The same tedious journey was repeated again with the same frequent halts. At one point we had to walk about half a mile along a road and past the door of a farmhouse. No one heard us. About three o'clock we arrived at the wood which I had planned for our final hide-out, but a quick reconnaissance of it showed it to be too dangerous to stay in. Though marked on the map as fairly thick, a lot of wood had been cut for charcoal and there were many freshly cut piles of timber and traces of men working. So I decided to retrace our steps about a mile and we finally came to rest in a small copse. This was by no means an ideal hide-out — as indeed none of them was — but the approach of daylight always limited any prolonged reconnaissance. Once again we hid the charges a little distance from ourselves and waited for the dawn to see how thick was the cover. Rain had been falling almost continuously so far.

It was soon light and the day was again spent in drying clothes and drawing water. We were in rather a public place as it was near a track junction and carts kept passing fairly regularly. There were men ploughing in the fields on both sides of us. About midday a dog suddenly barked near us and, following up our scent, ran in and found us in our clearing and stayed there barking. The farmer who owned him naturally came in to investigate the noise and discovered us all and asked us what we were doing there. H told him that we were fleeing from the Germans and he seemed fairly sympathetic and said that his son up in the north was also avoiding the *relève*. He also warned us of the Germans in Autun, but offered us no food or shelter. He may also have noticed certain curious items lying on the ground, such as our flasks and the tins of bully beef, though naturally the weapons were hidden. Such an accident was unavoidable and was a constant possibility. One could hide from men but not from dogs. In the end he went away again, and I decided we must move from the spot at the first opportunity at night.

In the afternoon we made up two sets of charges and packed them into a rucksack and an empty sandbag as I intended to take them with me that night on my reconnaissance and leave them up near the factory. This was the only method in which we could use the extra sets of charges, as it was impossible for one man to carry two sets of charges once they had been made up and we had set out on the attack. It was then that I discovered also that the buckle on about six out of the twenty-four charges had come off and, considering the flimsy way they had been put on in the first place, we might have had more trouble later. Fortunately we had some parachute cord with us and were able to patch them up again, but the whole matter was most unsatisfactory, as our resources, cut off from the outside world in a wood, were naturally very limited. Furthermore, the lettering on the charges was mis-spelt and, in some instances, put on the side that would have been against the wall and, therefore, impossible to read.

It rained all during this time, and we had to stop work from time to time whenever carts passed.

In the evening we moved forward again into the wood originally chosen for our final hide-out and by daylight I was able to find a corner of it that looked fairly uninhabited and that would be safe for the next day. I and D set off on our reconnaissance at nine forty-five p.m. taking the charges with us.

THE ATTEMPT FOILED

The route to the factory was very tortuous on account of the nature of the hedges, even though one was following the river all the way. We crossed over two bridges and the main country road and continued down to the target. On the right hand side was a line of farms dotted about fairly regularly about four hundred yards from the river, making a long gauntlet of about two miles altogether. The country-side was quiet and deserted; there was no sound on the roads and no dogs barking. As all the time to date, bar the first night, it was a typical tranquil countryside.

At the last field before the factory we stopped and squeezed the water out of our shoes. We also hid the ruck-sack with the charges in a ditch that was overgrown with a hedge and brambles. The place was in a corner of the hedge and the river, and in the dark the charges looked quite ade-quately concealed. We then continued on towards the plant, and after crawling the entire width of a field passed the tank farm and oil refinery on our right, and ended up under the first bridge and hid there for some time in the shadows. A few minutes earlier we had seen a man walk out of the factory along the bridge and then return again short-ly afterwards. As he was walking fairly fast I hoped he was not on guard, but we had to keep fairly quiet where we were in case he decided to walk back again overhead. From here, with the use of field glasses, one could get a good apprecia-tion of the target.

Firstly the whole oil plant was surrounded by a ten foot high wire fence which would have been impossible to cut with our wirecutters, for it was of thick close mesh. The only possible entrance was by following the railway over the bridge and in past the wooden gates in the perimeter of the factory. There was a sentry-box at the gate, but I do not think there was anyone inside that night and it was proba-bly only occupied in the day time.

The frequent running of the trucks up to the slag-heap had stopped at midnight and now there was only one every fifteen minutes. The retorts were covered over on top and it was possible to see the reflection of lights underneath. Out-side there were four hanging lights — one red, three white. I did not think that my reconnaissance justified an attempt to enter the factory that night, as one could not be certain that the sentry-box was vacant and the approach up to it was bound to be noisy. I had made my plan and, as it was after three o'clock, we withdrew.

On the way back we had to pass along the road. As we approached a house a dog barked and a light was flashed on almost at once, but we were past the door before anything else happened.

The following day passed as usual in intermittent rain. In the afternoon we made up the remainder of the charges. Towards evening two more dogs smelt us out and barked, but nobody appeared. The night, though as yet misty, looked like developing into full moonlight. I planned to collect the other two charges on the way and place them underneath the bridge, with the safety rings extracted and leaving the time pencils all ready to press on our way out. If we destroyed the railway in this fashion, we would have delayed for some days the transport of oil to the station. The rest of the party were then to wait under the bridge while I investigated the sentry-box, and, that being cleared, we would then enter and attack either two batteries of retorts or, if that was impossible, the conveyor.

We set out at nine forty-five following the river, but I noticed, on crossing the first bridge, that the gap in the hedge which I had forced the night before, seemed to have been filled in again. On approaching the second bridge and the main road, I suddenly noticed a man standing on the bridge with a light. We naturally stopped to observe and a few minutes later a bicycle patrol of four men passed one behind the other and were challenged by the sentry on the bridge. I left the party under cover and went forward alone to investigate further. On the far side of the road, where we had to pass, there were lights flashing in the fields and dogs barking in the farms. All this was in complete contrast to the night before when the countryside could not have been more tranquil. While I waited there, another patrol of four men on bicycles passed on the road. The sentry was there for the night.

It was obvious that the alarm had been given and it was

impossible to continue with the attack under such conditions. There was no other approach to the target that I knew, and we would have had to come back that way in any case as we had left our clothes and boots in the wood from which we started. Once a cordon was out it was suicidal to stay in that area, as our path through the hedges could be followed back to our hide-out.

The alarm may have been given either through the discovery of the first two charges, the talking of the farmer, suspicions aroused by the owner of the lighted house the night before, or some independent local reason which we had no means of finding out.

I had previously decided that that must be the final night of the operation as we had no more food, except for our emergency escape ration, and I did not consider that the men, although completely confident up to now, could hang about indefinitely under those weather conditions.

I decided there was no alternative but to abandon the operation. We buried the charges in the wood and I ordered the party to Paris. As it was, when H and I finally arrived there after a lot of walking three nights later, we were on the verge of exhaustion and had had nothing to eat, except a tin of bully beef and a handful of biscuits between us, for the last forty-eight hours. I myself remained in bed at Paris and Lyons until the time came to cross the Pyrenees.

There follows a reference to some 'notes in France'. A few references pencilled on a separate sheet seem to be the notes referred to. Jean Moulin, one of the leaders of the French resistance, was arrested in a suburb of Lyons on the 21st of June, two months later. The narrative begins again with the crossing of the Pyrenees from Perpignan.

FIRST CROSSING OF THE PYRENEES

The train arrived in Perpignan about nine o'clock in the morning, and we passed the day rather interminably sitting about in the park, eating in indifferent restaurants and sleeping in the cinema, while H contacted the guides.

Always in the distance were the cloud-capped Pyrenees — a constant reminder of the evening's ordeal. At seven-thirty we got into a bus, crammed already with returning villagers, and drove out along the flat winding roads for a mile and a half to the village of X, where our walking began. As we finally came opposite and underneath the actual peak which we were to cross, the sight of its towering outline against the evening sky filled me with awe and dread. I had put my legs up on a ledge in the bus and as soon as we got out they felt miserably weak. I thought I would never make those mountains, but there was no other hope.

We set out along the road leading to the foothills, following a man on a bicycle who was our first guide. We walked fast because the light was failing. After half an hour we suddenly turned off the main road and followed a sunken track to the right. Behind a tree a man with a stick who looked rather like a shepherd was waiting. We sat down for a few minutes in a ditch and adjusted our shoes before setting off finally. The man on the bicycle turned back, and we followed the second guide. The first hour was easy going across fields and vine-yards, along sunken paths and hedges and the beds of streams. We crossed two main roads and, as the sun set, we entered the wooded country of the foothills. Here the going became steeper, but always there was a path of some sort, or a gap in the hedge. The vineyards were now terraced, and our feet often slipped in the loose rubble and stones. We walked up the drive leading to a farm, and then climbed up a steep bank of undergrowth to the left. The slope was increasing rapidly, and already my legs were weary. Every time we stopped for a moment the strain was broken, and the mental tension as of a spring slipped, and I was conscious again of my weakness. An hour later I had passed beyond that stage, and had ceased any longer to draw on my reserve of physical strength, and only obeyed the dictates of my will. I no longer felt fatigue because I was

living on my nerves. As long as the rhythm of my mind
continued I knew I could endure until I dropped, but I
knew that, once that tension was relaxed, the reaction
would be severe. Five minutes after entering the consulate
in Barcelona three days later at the end of my journey my
voice suddenly went completely and I could not utter a single word; my two companions only exhausted their bodies,
but I had already passed beyond that stage after the third
hour of the first night.

Now we reached a rough stone path which led vertically
up towards the heights. Here we sat down and, stringing our
boots round our necks, put on espadrilles. Our guide said we
should reach the crest in two hours' time, by one a.m. The
last stage of the ascent was beginning.

Soon the track ended and henceforward it was all rocks
and boulders and trailing thorns which tripped one up. By
now it was pitch dark, and no moon or stars. I could just
distinguish the faint colour of the raincoat of the man two
yards in front of me. If I delayed for an instant at the crossing of a ledge, even that vanished and one was in danger of
losing the way altogether. It was impossible to see where
one's feet were going and in the dark one misjudged dis-
tances and either plunged wildly or stubbed one's toes
against the rocks. My ankles were always twisting as the
rope sandals gave them no support at all. Once or twice
they made me wince momentarily, and my constant dread
was that I should slip and sprain them. Last month our
guide had brought over the mountains a man with a broken
leg, and I can imagine no worse nightmare.

Looking back one saw the lights of Perpignan miles
behind. The air was sharp; it was nearly one o'clock. We
averaged, I should think, about four paces a minute. Suddenly the goat track ended abruptly against a boulder. The
guide stopped and searched about a little, and then admitted he was lost. A think mist was coming down, our clothes
were wet with rain, and the ground was slippery.

Our guide decided we were too much to the left on the

wrong peak, so down we plunged again through the trees. Time was passing and we were still some way from the frontier and dawn was only three hours away. We were all very weary. In the dense mist the guide switched on his torch to help me find the right path, and off we set again at a terrible pace. The first two men were all right because they could use the light of the torch, but at the back I could see nothing and struggled desperately to keep up. We were walking sideways along the slope and every minute one of us fell. I know of no experience so exasperating and tempting to despair as that next half hour, falling and getting up again, running where we could to catch up, unseen branches striking our heads and eyes, and all the time our guide urging us to hurry. Still we were lost and kept on retracing our steps, and to my mind going in a circle — now uphill — now downhill. The thought of losing all that height laboriously gained was heartbreaking.

I wondered whether the German patrols and observation posts on the crest would see the torch. Even in the mist its light seemed terribly naked under the dark of the trees. If it was seen I suppose a machine gun might have opened fire, or dogs been sent out to detect us and bark our presence till the patrols arrived. There would be no killing or losing the dogs.

H took out his compass and showed it to the guide who did not understand it and was very insulted. He followed his paths by memory and recognition; there was no other way and direction did not matter. In that thick mist I could not blame him for losing the way and it was almost miraculous that he ever found it again. But find it he did at the end of an hour, and up we went again towards the summit. We crept past an unoccupied German post ten yards away. Descending the far slope we hit the main frontier road and walked down it for a mile. Then we turned off it and down to the bed of a stream which was to be the rendezvous with the Spanish guide. Here we were left for half an hour while our first guide went off to contact his friend. My sceptical

companions, who had suffered from the treachery of the
frontier guides before, doubted he would ever return. But
back he came with his companion, and brought also some
bread and figs. We had been told we would be taken to a
farm in Spain where we could sleep and eat the following
day, but now suddenly at four a.m., dead tired, we learned
that no such farm existed at all. We had no food or shelter
and would have to walk the whole way on to Figueras; it
was not a pleasant discovery.

Off we set again and by some perversity of mountain
paths had to climb all the way back again past the road and
up to the topmost crest once more. Here, after a final terrible argument over money, our French guide left us and
returned. Light was just breaking and we quickly covered
the last ascent into Spain.

Day showed us a rocky plateau with more ranges between
us and the Spanish lowland and behind the snow-capped
peaks of highest Pyrenees. We had ascended nearly four
thousand feet from sea level and had been climbing without
stop for ten hours. The dawn wind in the hills was chilly
and there was no point in stopping to rest as sleep in that
cold was impossible and our clothes were wringing wet. By
the morning we must be the far side of the next range as
the Spanish guards would come up the valley to post the
sentries on the crest. Our guide told us that for him capture
would mean death, but for us only imprisonment. The
observation posts along the frontier kept a constant watch
with telescope on the mountain tracks, and any movement
was at once noticed and followed up, so in deference to his
repeated urging we dragged ourselves down the valley and
up the other side and collapsed finally and completely on a
rocky ledge. Far below us we could hear the tinkle of cattle
bells and the sounds of work in the fields. The sun was shining on France.

Already we had lost all confidence in our new guide and
talked about him among ourselves in the most contemptuous terms. He, being Catalan, understood not a word of

ours, nor we him. Conversation was impossible and fatigue lent an edge to our indignation; for the last three hours he had continuously led us up and down the ridges of ravines when he could have followed the crestline all the time. He was also leading us steadily away from Spain. Actually, as we discovered later, he had excellent and irrefutable reasons for doing this, and was in fact the best guide I have ever met. But at this stage we distrusted him profoundly and debated whether we should abandon him completely and strike out on our own. I refused to believe his story of the guards in those silent mountains and continued to talk at the top of my voice. Like typical Englishmen we took out the compasses again and pointed to the sun, explaining arrogantly where was the east and where was Spain. My companions, who had travelled that way already, were even more outspoken than I.

Pedro, as we christened him, was almost beside himself with anger and kept on demanding who was the guide. Later on we came to realize that he knew from childhood every blade of grass on those hills and knew more about field-craft from years of experience than we should ever have guessed. His contempt of us was one hundred times deeper and better justified than ours for him, and we soon put away the compasses and obeyed him implicitly.

This Spanish ruffian, whose language no one could understand, was completely lord and master, and I accepted his most terrible abuse and disapproval. He picked on me as the permanent scapegoat and, if any of us did anything wrong, his displeasure and rebuke were at once vented against me. I could only weep in silent rage and swore that just as soon that we got to Barcelona, I would kick his teeth out in the street. And yet, for all that, I liked and respected Pedro, and, though like all Spaniards money was his only motive, yet he was a brave man who faced these mountains and their risks, sometimes three times a week, and underneath our mutual contempt there was a strong bond of mutual affection. Three days later he shook my hand very warmly in Barcelona when the time came to say good-bye.

As the mist had lifted Pedro permitted us the luxury of a fire which he conjured himself out of wet twigs in a way that was truly miraculous. He was clearly a first-rate scout. He gave us some of his wine and a slice of sausage each and, as always with the morning and the warmth, hope returned. We lay by the fire and tried to describe to Pedro the sensation of a bombing raid. This he enjoyed immensely, except when we raised the pitch of our voices. We were all for continuing our journey, but Pedro would not hear of it till dark, and all our pleading could not induce him to move before five o'clock.

We slept intermittently and woke up at midday to find Pedro had vanished. We were at once plunged into gloom as everyone presumed that he had run away and left us through fear of the mountain guards. However, finding we still had our money and wallets on us, I was certain he had not and, sure enough, five minutes later he jumped down from behind a rock where he too had been sleeping in private.

We set off again in the evening and, after crossing the last crest, looked down through the gaps in the clouds on the sun-lit fields of Spain. That view from the Pyrenees, with the sea on our left and the mountains all around us, and the driving mist to give a sense of perspective and distance, was an unforgettable experience. To be back on a decent downhill path again was also pleasant. After two hours we came to the first belt of habitation and here in a ruined church we rested till nightfall. Once more Pedro, like the djinn he was, produced a roaring fire that nearly set the roof alight, and once more we dried our clothes. The leaping flames and the darkness outside reminded me of Christmas and hypnotized us into forgetting the future and the past; staring into a fire makes one like an ostrich burying its head in the sand; within that circle all is safety and comfort. The church had a stone terrace and winding steps that led us down into the valley beneath. A fountain of water ran unceasingly while everything was deserted and in ruins. By one a.m. we were down on the level land at last. An hour before in the thick undergrowth Pedro had lost the way, but presently found it again. To untrained eyes there was not even flattened grass or worn stones to distinguish the way through the wilderness, and every ten minutes we passed by mazes of track junctions. In the pitch dark it was impossible to see even the man in front, let alone any markings on the ground. Yet on we had gone for three days now and only twice had he lost the route.

We now came out on the main road and Pedro hurried us along it towards Figueras. He was naturally terrified of patrols and the pace he set was cruel. All the time the rain poured down, and we splashed ankle-deep in the puddles on the road. Every now and again the huge lights of a car would flash in the sky ahead and we would throw ourselves flat behind the trees and hedges on the side as it passed. After two hours of this six-mile-an-hour walking, we turned off the main road and followed different cart tracks until we came finally to another ruined barn which was to be our home for the night. The door was shut behind and, deadbeat, we threw ourselves down on the floor, while Pedro made a fire out of the dripping wood, and the smoking fumes choked and blinded us until we could hardly bear it. At five a.m. H got up and sent Pedro off into the village to get some food. He promised he would be back without fail by nine-o'clock.

Midday came and showed no signs of Pedro, and once more we were in despair. This time we had made the mistake of giving him some money and it seemed he had little incentive to return; in any case there could be no reason for his delay. All hope of food or Barcelona faded and we tried to get some sleep to forget our hunger. At one o'clock Pedro suddenly reappeared in the doorway with a punctured bicycle and a rucksack full of oranges, bananas, bread, omelettes and a bottle of milk. It was the best meal I have ever had in my life and our happiness could know no higher limits. We were sheltered from the wind and the afternoon passed in a haze of content, while Pedro returned by train to Barcelona to arrange a taxi for the night. Life was certainly worthwhile.

At sunset we were sitting beside the hut drinking in the peace of the deserted vineyard, while I tried to find some laces for my espadrilles. Suddenly the dark face of Pedro appeared around the corner and took us unawares. He swore that he could hear us talking a mile away, and for the next ten minutes he unleashed his anger and abuse on my head. I could not help but laugh, thinking back to the incongruous days of Warminster barracks[1], but this of course only made Pedro wilder still.

We set off once more in the dusk and, after we had been walking for a few minutes, another shape loomed up out of the hedge. I thought it was the Civic Guard, but it turned out to be a most extraordinary apparition. It had a white shirt and trousers rolled up to the knees and walked bare-foot like some enormous frog. The man spoke French and Spanish perfectly and had a great air of ease as befitted a man of the world. Pedro in comparison looked nothing but an illiterate peasant. The newcomer was apparently the head of the Spanish organization and was clearly the arch-bandit of the Pyrenees. He reminded me of Lob in *Dear Brutus*.

He accompanied us for the rest of the night and I could hardly take me eyes off him for fascination. I was afraid he might vanish into thin air. Last week one of the chiefs of the French organization had been caught on this last stage of the journey by the police, and they wanted to find out what prison he had been taken to, so that they could get him out. The guide on that occasion had of course got away, and, when we asked who had been the guide, Lob

---

[1] The 2nd Battalion of the Irish Guards were training at Warminster barracks when Hugh Dormer left to join SOE. They then moved to Shaker's Wood, Norfolk, to Duncombe Park in Yorkshire and finally to Brighton just before the invasion of France.

replied with a laugh that he had been.

Our field-craft had by now rather degenerated. Lob strode on in front his voice booming over the fields and Pedro sulked behind pushing his bicycle, whose chain kept coming off. Just ahead of us were the lights of Figueras. We came to a river and taking off our boots splashed nicely through it, knee-deep. The water was wonderfully cool and reflected the stars and the young moon. Crickets were humming in the grass. It might have been an African night.

We crossed the main road and, striking uphill, skirted the fort of Figueras on the hill. D had been imprisoned there on his last journey, so we gave it a wide berth. Passing under a viaduct we made a circular sweep to the south of the town, walking across fields and vineyards. Lob went on in front to make certain that the coast was clear, as they did not want to repeat their mistake. He would go ahead about four hundred yards and then flash his torch to give us the direction. We crossed two more streams and suddenly found ourselves entering a village. It was about one a.m., and we were very tired. Pedro ordered us to pick up our feet so as not to kick any loose stones. D behind me was stumbling and making a dreadful noise when suddenly Pedro darted back, came straight for me, seized my arm and shook it angrily like a dog. I tried to beat him off with a stick and a row soon ensued in the middle of the village street. A dog started barking, so we left off our argument and continued rapidly.

At last we came out on the main Barcelona road and, lying down behind a hay wagon, we waited for the taxi to arrive. The organization was wonderful, for within five minutes the headlights flashed on the road and we were hurriedly tumbled into the back seats of the car. I had cut myself a rather useful stick, but Pedro, just as he was closing the door, caught sight of it and threw it out. At this time I was too tired even to protest.

The next three hours reached the utmost realms of the fantastic. The three of us lay exhausted in the back, aching with hunger and thirst, while Pedro and Lob sat in front of

us eating eggs and drinking flasks of wine. They were exul-
tant with success, and it would never have entered their
heads to offer us anything. Pedro kept on squeezing my
knee and laughing uproariously and making noises, which
one could only presume were meant to represent the sound
of bombs bursting from aeroplanes. I swore back at him, but
of course he never understood a word. In front another
Spaniard drove in typical fashion while his mistress, who I
presume had been brought on the journey to lend an air of
respectability, leant her head on his shoulder and distracted
his attention from the steering wheel. Thereupon everyone
else in the car gradually fell asleep until even Pedro became
alarmed and, as we approached each corner, used to call out
and hit the driver on the head to make sure he was still
awake. The tyres slithered and screamed round the bends
until, as was only inevitable sooner or later, we had a punc-
ture. I felt myself slip slowly into the realms of madness,
like Alice in Wonderland, and expected any minute to
wake up again on the parade ground at Warminster before a
battalion of guardsmen.

To change the wheel we stopped in the main street of a
town. Everything was brilliantly lit up by electric lamps,
and two cars that passed stopped and offered their assistance. Pedro ran after the first one, holding on to the door
handle to prevent anyone getting out, and this frightened
the occupants into continuing their journey; ours must
have seemed an odd reaction to their Samaritan senti-
ments. The other one must have been a friend of Lob's, as
we heard him admitting in his off-hand manner that he had
three 'Inglese' in the back. We of course sat where we were
inside, our weight thus making it almost impossible to
change the wheel; the jack broke three times. The driver's
mistress got out and foolishly allowed the light from the
street lamps to fall on her face. The time was about four
a.m. What any passing policeman would have thought of it
all I shudder to think, especially as by now we were completely blocking the road. But Lob would have explained it

away. He could explain away anything. He nearly explained Pedro's money away which he owed him as our guide.

This operation took nearly an hour. When everybody had climbed in again, we resumed the journey. At the next village there was a control, so the car was stopped before it and we got out and walked around the outskirts of the town and climbed back into the car again at the other side. The next control we rushed, which was perfectly safe as the guard was fast asleep inside his sentry-box, and did not even hear the car pass. A little farther on Lob got out and vanished into the darkness at the entrance to Barcelona; Pedro was paid and also left us. The farewell scene was really rather touching. I was too tired to fulfil my promise to kick his teeth out and in any case it was almost light.

For an extra two hundred pesetas the driver consented to hide us in his garage till the consulate opened at nine a.m. Here, locked in like rats, we passed the next three hours tidying up. I washed the mud off my boots and plastered my hair down with water out of the radiator.

At nine o'clock we set out again and, after a rather unpleasant ten minutes waiting in the street outside, H went in and got one of the secretaries to escort us past the patrols in the entrance into the consulate. We walked up three flights of stairs and crossed the threshold into safety at last. The long journey was over; five minutes later I was incapable of uttering even a whisper.

SPAIN AND THE JOURNEY TO LISBON

Here in Barcelona I spent the next five days as the guest of the Consul-General[1], who had been in the Coldstream Guards in the last war, and whose son I had known in the Armoured Division. My boots had split down the side and I was given a new pair of brown shoes and lent a typically English tweed suit. After a bath and hair-cut and a square meal and twelve hour's sleep I was transformed back again

[1] H L Farquhar M.C.

into a guardsman.

During the siesta hour I lay on my bed and read Arthur Koestler's account of six months in Seville prison during the Spanish Civil War, when he had been condemned to death and every night some thirty out of the two thousand prisoners were executed; and he told of how at midnight the warder and the priest used to come down the dark passages with a candle and a tinkling bell and knock on the cell doors of those who were to die that night, and how the ritual was always the same with the warders saying quietly, '*Valor, hombre! Venga!* — Courage, man ! Come!' *Hombre* — *ecce homo* — behold this man! At such times only the simple words have sufficient force and nobility to meet the occasion — *Valor, hombre! Venga!* — and, as Koestler truly remarked, it is not death but the act of dying that frightens men.

In the evening I went to the English hospital and chatted to a Maltese sailor of forty-six, who had been brought over the mountains with a broken leg. The inhumanity of the Spanish prisons he had previously been in was indescribable. Men in wintertime, arriving with frostbitten limbs, were left unattended for days until they got gangrene, and what doctors there were used no anaesthetics and all their operations had to be opened again at Barcelona. Prison life leaves its mark on men for life; it hardens and crushes even more often than it ennobles.

The Consul-General took me down to his house on the sea for the weekend, and here I rested on the veranda all day while the unchanging sea thundered below as on the old quay at Cannes long ago, while I lay in bed at night with the windows open; so loud was the roaring of the waves that I expected them to come foaming into the room at any moment. There is no more soothing music to the nerves than the rhythm of the sea, and I think that, had it not been for the kindness of my hosts, I might have taken weeks to recover from the fatigue of my travels. The civilizing influence of Diplomatic dinners and silver and servants was a perfect antidote to the rough manners of Pedro and the Pyrenees.

On the fifth day we started early in the morning and drove the six hundred kilometres to Madrid, which was the next stage of our journey home. The journey took ten hours and was very interesting. The scenery changed continually, from the blue Catalan hills to begin with, passing through Lerida and the flat Mexican desert, straight on to Saragossa and finally the last stretch on to Madrid. The countryside seemed arid and deserted; vines were the only form of cultivation and all the time the blue skies were cloudless under the sun. We stopped for lunch on the roadside and there was not a breath of wind. The nearest we ever came to death in the whole five weeks since leaving England was when I misjudged a bend in the cliff's face and nearly drove the car over the edge.

We reached Madrid by evening and I went to the house of the Naval Attaché[1], which was high up and had a terrace which commanded a fine view of the city. The next evening he gave a big dinner party for Leslie Howard.

On Sunday I heard High Mass at Saint Bernardino's; the Benedictine Plain Chant made me very homesick. Afterwards I went to the Prado and saw Goya for the first time. In the evening at five-thirty p.m. I went to my first bull fight and my last one. If I were a Spaniard I should want to be a matador, for there is no denying it is a brave man's job, but to be a spectator is only cruel and sickly.

The time came to leave Madrid. We drove by night and reached Seville about ten a.m. I drove from midnight till four o'clock, while the other slept. The car was a Ford V8, and I was touching seventy miles an hour most of the way. I know of no greater exhilaration than to drive fast at night, when one mistake will hurl all the sleeping passengers to instant destruction.

On reaching Seville I learnt that I had to complete the rest of the journey to Lisbon on foot. I spent that day and the night in a crowded house in a back street. In the same

[1] Captain A H Hillgarth C.M.G., O.B.E., M.C.

house were four French sailors who had escaped from Toulon when their submarine had been sunk. The family consisted of about fifteen, who came and went perpetually. In the afternoon the heat was stifling and I escaped on to the roof, where there were some geraniums in pots and a broken terrace and the open sky.

The airless clouds twisted into a funnel of heat. My homeland seemed somehow farther away than it had ever been these last few weeks. In the evening after dinner we went out for a walk at midnight. People were sitting on their doorsteps and dancing in the open squares. The narrow streets of Seville and the old walls of the Alcazar and the gardens and the street lamps all belong to another world. The cathedral and its Moorish tower were silhouetted against the cloudless sky; the full moon looked down through the palm trees.

The next day passed monotonously again, as in a prison. One moved one's chair round the roof to escape the sun, until at midday there was no longer any shadow at all and one was driven below until the evening.

At eight p.m. I set off for Lisbon in company with the four French sailors who were lodging with me. They had previously escaped from a prison in the north of Spain after wading through a marsh up to their necks and being fired at by the guards. Half of their party had been killed or re-caught, and the police were looking for the others. To live in the company of escaped prisoners and Reds and desperate men had no longer become the normal life for me, and I was beginning to feel dreadfully homesick for an English drawing room again and my mother's conversation. Our guide got quite worried when such thoughts came into my mind and asked the others in Portuguese why the 'Inglese' was so 'triste'. Among these people I felt as alone as Talbot among the Eskimos[†] in the lands of the Archipelago, and yet he could not even speak their language, while I could at least understand what these said.

† Talbot Clifton. See *The Book of Talbot* by Violet Clifton..

We set off in a ramshackle taxi from the main square in Seville and drove for two hours towards the frontier. We passed through several villages thronged with children and people in the lighted streets. The guide sat in the front waving and shouting greetings to the patrols who were passing on the roadside — some of them, I gathered, were also in the business.

We got out of the taxi about ten-thirty p.m. at the outskirts of a village and started walking around it, following cart tracks. The going was fairly easy and absolutely flat.

We followed paths through the fields standing high for the harvest. At midnight we rested for an hour. I lay on my back and stared up at the sky. The ears of corn glistened against the moonlight and the scent of the fields was everywhere. Each such moment seemed unique, for in a few moments we were moving on again and that experience could never be recaptured.

At three o'clock we approached a town and followed round it along the railway. The dogs were barking on all sides. We came to a long iron bridge spanning a river and passed over it on tiptoe, as there was a guard at the farther end. But all went well and daylight found us in a wood.

As usual the mirage of houses and food, promised us in Seville, turned out to be non-existent. For the next three hours we went aimlessly up and down the valleys, as our guide had lost the way. We ended up finally by the overgrown bed of a river, where at last we could drink. The guide went off in search of food and at two o'clock returned with some bread and cheese and my gourd full of wine. I could not face the Spanish sausages, which were red and rancid in the sun. Afterwards we slept.

At seven p.m. we moved on again and found that that was the best time for walking. It was still light and cool and there was a great peace at the hour of sunset which no words can fitly express. All the fields and their poppies and the vineyards were still; we and the browsing herds were the only living things in that landscape. We covered only a few kilometres that night as our guide had to return to collect another party from Seville. We spent the night in a small thatched hut with two goats in a corresponding state of uncleanliness. There was something warm in a pot to eat, which I much appreciated. As I lay in the dark on the reeds in this minute hut, which could just hold five men, life again seemed very bizarre. One of the Frenchmen lit his pipe and the match showed the head of the goat sniffing curiously at the flame, which was a sight for a painting.

At daylight we withdrew and lay up till evening in the shade of a fig tree. Outside the sun burned down mercilessly under the blue sky. This country has much more in common with Africa than Europe and seemed very remote from my memories of Salisbury Plain. Flies and mosquitoes buzzed around us incessantly and sleep was impossible. I was tired of travelling.

After dinner I cheered up, as another Englishman and four Poles arrived in the second party. The Poles were all charming and had epic stories of their escape. One, a boy of seventeen, had left Warsaw penniless and had worked his way all through Europe to the Pyrenees. He had crossed the Spanish frontier by wading along the coastline in the sea, and then he had walked from Hendaye to Madrid. He was now in a pitiful condition, with emaciated body and pale face. Another was an infantry officer who had fought in the Polish war against the Germans and had afterwards escaped to Marseilles via Yugoslavia, Roumania, Turkey, Syria, Beirut, and Alexandretta. It had taken him over a year. If the war lasted for another year, he said, Poland would be a desert for ever. The Germans had killed five million civilians altogether. The third was a man of forty-seven, who had formerly been a professor at a university and spoke five languages. He had escaped from an internment camp packed inside a gramophone box in the back of a lorry and labelled by himself to 'Miss Moore, British Embassy, Madrid', where he duly arrived after being sick inside the box with the jolting of the lorry. It must have seemed a far cry from the peace of his university days to trudging over these Spanish hills. They were all Catholics and wore medals around their necks and were full of confidence.

We lay up under the fig trees talking all afternoon. At four p.m. the Spanish guide stole my leather gourd, which hitherto had been invaluable. One was completely in their hands, so one could say nothing.

We set off walking again at ten p.m., and again it was easy going along fields. My English companion said it reminded him of the International Brigade as we had a Spaniard, a Portuguese, four Poles, two Englishmen and four Frenchmen. Any messages were passed from the guide to the other Englishman in Spanish. He translated them to me in English. I translated them into French and the professor passed them on finally in Polish.

At three-thirty a.m. the guide got tired, so we just had to put up for the night in some thick undergrowth till morning. At daylight we discovered a river and washed our clothes and shaved in it.

Again the day passed slowly in trying to find a little shade among the bushes and constantly changing one's position to avoid the pitiless sun as it moved across the sky. Flies and ants were very troublesome. I went and lay beside the professor and we had a long talk in French about books and history. Our conversation ranged from Spengler to the *Seven Pillars*, and Plato, and Napoleon, and the Congress of Vienna, and Poland in 1939. It all reminded me of Socrates *au bord de la rivière*. He had lived thirty years in Paris and was a true citizen of the world. He had passed ten terrible months in a German concentration camp by the Pyrenees. A friend of his had recently been made a general under Giraud in North Africa and wanted him to go out and join his Staff when he arrived. He had a very cheerful and cultured mind and showed me a wooden statue of Our Lady which he had carried with him all the way from Poland. It was beautifully carved.

I talked also with the young Pole of seventeen who had

left Warsaw without a penny and had worked his way across
Europe via Berlin, Vienna, Holland, Belgium and France.
He had worked for three months at Lorient, and said that
the destruction dealt there by the R.A.F. to the submarine
base was indescribable. One night he had been in a shelter
there during an air raid, when it received a direct hit. Of
the eighty-four occupants he and three others were the only
people not killed. Had he not been drunk that night, the
experience would have driven him mad. He told me how
the very first Sunday of the Polish war the German planes
had come over and machine-gunned the church proces-
sions from twenty feet, which had been a terrible sight.
Later he spoke of the siege of Warsaw in which, as he
expressed it, he had had the honour to take part. Later he
had served for a time in the Russian army. What memories
these men must have! I should think there have been few
finer examples of unflinching faith and patriotism.

We ate some bread and cheese at six and lay around
under the bushes afterwards smoking and talking in five
languages, till it was dark enough to set out. The French
sailors recounted how their submarine had been hit and
severely damaged by an American bomber at the time of
the North African landings; how they tried to set sail and
set out for Casablanca, but this had been impossible and
they had been forced to sabotage it at Cadiz. When they
escaped through the marshes outside the prison the
Spaniards did not believe it possible and were still dredging
the place for their bodies. At times they had floundered in
the mud up to their necks.

We moved off at eight o'clock while the sun was still
high. After an hour we had to lie up for a time in a field till
it grew dark enough to pass a village. I lay on my back and
nibbled the ears of corn. Then on we went again for the
next eight hours up into the hills. The moon did not rise till
midnight and till then the valleys were dark. Above us
shone the brilliant planets Venus and Jupiter, and behind
Aquila with its red star Altair; Vega and Arcturus and the

Pole Star marked their nightly triangle. I regarded all the
myriad constellations of the sky as fellow travellers and
found them very comforting. Time passed quickly in their
company. I slept on the rock strewn hillside from five to six
and woke cold and desolate in the naked moonlight. We
pushed on quickly again to arrive before full morning. Two
hours later we stopped finally half-way down a cliff face on a
rocky ledge overlooking the valley and the river beneath.
There was a wonderful view west towards Portugal and the
blue hills in the distance. I was delighted to discover three
pairs of golden eagles nesting among the trees, which
showed how desolate the place was. The air was full of the
dawn chorus of the birds and the cooing of doves was
repeated like a strange echo from the opposite side of the
valley. We made a fire and warmed our hands and ate some
bread. Afterwards, when the sun had got up a little, we went
down to the swift flowing river and, stripping completely,
bathed in the warm water and washed our clothes. There
were shoals of tiny fish which nibbled at one's body. One of
the French sailors sat on the bank and tried to tickle trout.
There was a shrub with a red flower which grew on the side.

Afterwards I climbed up on to the ledge and slept till
midday in the shade of the cool rocks. It was an enchanting
valley and I would have willingly sat there for weeks. It
made all the fatigue of our long walk well worth while. In
the evening I sat up in our eyrie and watched the golden
eagles wheeling for hours above the valley. They soared
over the trees without any movement of their wings catch-
ing the currents of air, and every now and then the sun
flashed on the brown of their bodies as they turned. They
must have been hunting for food for their young. I thought
back to the days of Queen Fann and Guardsman McGee[1].

At night we set out on the last stage and would cross the

[1] Queen Fann was a peregrine falcon which Hugh Dormer had when he
was with the 2nd battalion on Salisbury Plain. Guardsman McGee, his
batman, was greatly attached to the falcon.

frontier between two posts five kilometres apart. If we ran
into a patrol of Spanish guards we would take them with us
to Lisbon, as we were ten and should outnumber them.
There is always a certain amount of nervous tension when
it comes to the actual moment of crossing frontiers, and for
the Poles to-night would be the climax of a year's journey. I
took a buttonhole from the red flowering shrub and we set
off about eight p.m. For the next two hours we walked west
into the setting sun with the trees standing out dark against
the sky and Venus the only star visible in the twilight. In
the distance was the tinkling of goat bells and the barking
of dogs. The breeze blew cool in our faces. We stopped and
asked some water of a peasant woman who was just settling
down for the night with her babies in a field. She had no
protection whatsoever, but was just sleeping in the open
amongst the corn. The poverty of these people is terrible,
for a people not even at war. While we drank out of a stone
pitcher, the children and the woman watched us like gipsies. Then we went on again. The going now was rough and
rocky and reminiscent of part of the Pyrenees, across
ploughed fields, down stone-strewn valleys with no path,
and we often stumbled in the dark. We passed between two
sets of lights on either hand, pausing often to listen, and
crossed the main road on tiptoe.

As the hours passed one lost oneself in the constant
rhythm of walking, till every action became automatic and
the mind soared out from the tired body, either into the
fields of memory or into the realms of imagination, and
then one knew one was asleep. I found myself back again in
the peaceful routine of the Benedictine School and
Monastery at Ampleforth, or at Oxford, or in the Irish
Guards. Sometimes one would walk on like that alone with
one's distant thought and then suddenly the mind would
revert with a start to the dark file of men threading their
way through the vineyards in the silence of the starlit sky,
and one could not think for a moment what one was doing
in such a scene. Again at halts I would throw myself down

again on the ground and be instantly asleep, and wake later cold and shivering in the wind and completely lost as to where I was or what I was doing there.

However, the route went on up and down hills, crossing rivers over stepping-stones, along slippery, rocky ledges. About midnight the moon came up over the hills round and crimson, but in the valleys it was still dark; we were hurrying quickly to cross the frontier before it was fully up. The guide had said we had only fifteen kilometres to walk, but it turned out to be thirty. The professor was in a terrible condition and could hardly stumble along; next morning his feet were shocking to see, all blistered and septic. The walk must have been an agony for him and was a complete triumph of the mind over the body, which, perhaps, comes more easily to a man of intellect, however academic his past.

So on we went into the night till we were dropping with exhaustion. At long last, at three in the morning, we came to a hilltop and looked down on the river which was the Portuguese frontier. We took off our shoes and socks and, rolling up our trousers, waded knee-deep through the water running cool and clear over the stones. We sat down on the far side and looked back at the dark valley in shadow and the moon shining on the river. Except for the angry croaking of bull-frogs there was the complete silence of the middle night; it was all very strange and fantastic.

Then we continued again, and, stumbling up a hill, came fifteen minutes later to our final resting place for the night — the hut of one of the other guides. We entered, all ten of us, and collapsed on the chairs, while the man and his wife lit a fire and made some excellent black coffee. The flame from the oil wick flickered on the thatched roof and the stone floor with just a bed and cupboard in the corner. It was a typical contrabandier's cabin and no doubt the guides combined such traffic with their other business of bringing us across the frontier. The woman, with a plain smock and blue shawl round her hair and holding a pitcher of water against her hip, looked like an Egyptian. Outside the door shone the moonlit night. The whole scene was unforgettable. Afterwards we were taken to the cowshed, where I slept with the Poles and some chickens on the stone floor.

In the morning we had some more coffee and hard bread and cheese, and spent the rest of the day in the shade while the frontier guards patrolled the hills outside. The Frenchman slept in the hayrick. I was beginning to find all this enforced inactivity and rest very tiring. It had something of a prison routine about it. One could not lie for long on the stone floor without getting sore and one could not talk above a whisper for fear of being heard outside. The sunlight entered through the chinks in the mud wall. At two o'clock we had a bowl of soup with bread in it and afterwards some potatoes and pieces of meat, also some white wine, which was civilization indeed. After lunch F went next door to discuss some business with the guides and was caught there by a neighbour who suddenly called in. He had to sit in a corner with a hat over his eyes and pretend to be asleep. In the evening we shaved, brushed our clothes and cleaned our shoes and had a last meal at nine. Another visitor delayed our departure by suddenly arriving on a horse and we had to lie motionless next door and listen through the chinks in the wall. It took a little time before one discovered whether it was the frontier guards or not.

Just before leaving at ten o'clock the wife came in and said good-bye to us and wished us luck. She had four brothers who were all guides, and it must have been lonely work living, often alone, in this hut on the frontier up in the hills and far from any village, and having to get up in the middle of the night to receive her nocturnal visitors. Once she had walked with her brother all three stages of our journey in a single night; she was a regular gipsy. She had been very charming to us and kept her house very clean and, as she waved us good-bye, when we set off, I was once more reminded of that Egyptian resemblance.

For the last time we set out over the hills and soon Spain

was lost to view in the dark. After two hours we came out on a road where two mule carts were waiting for us, just outside the frontier zone. I got into the first one with the Poles and for the next four hours we had a mad ride to the station as our guide thought we were late and would miss the train, which only runs once every twenty-four hours. It was very cramped and hard bunched up on the bottom of the cart, and at every bend on the slope they would whip up the mules into a mad gallop, until I thought the cart would overturn or lose one of its creaking wheels; in either case it would have meant instant death. At the top of the next hill our cart stopped and the one behind continued dashing blindly on into the back of ours and the professor, who was sitting on the tailboard, had the job of fending it off. Half the time we rode with the other mule's head almost in the back of our cart.

With typical Spanish unreliability our guide suddenly decided we had plenty of time to catch the train, and indeed we eventually arrived at the station an hour in advance; so we stopped in the next village and woke up the innkeeper and bought some fire-water and cognac. Our guide and the man guiding the horses rapidly proceeded to get drunk on the contents and the rest of the journey was absolute babel. They sang at the top of their voices, standing up in the swaying cart — especially one tune called 'Lirra Tirra' which occurred very regularly. One of the men had a good voice and sang Portuguese folk songs and pretended to accompany himself on a guitar, and in this confusion we rode on through the sleeping countryside until we finally arrived at the station about four a.m.

As we had a long time to wait we went and knocked up another friend of the guide who gave us more coffee and cognac. He looked a proper Mexican bandit with an enormous paunch and a sombrero hat. His wife squatted in a black shawl and fanned the fire in the middle of the floor. At five o'clock the train arrived and we had a seven-hour journey to Lisbon, changing only once. The third class carriage was packed with Portuguese all eating and very hot. There was a man who played a mandoline in the corner. The train stopped at every single station. I felt dirty and disgusted and thought the journey would never end.

At midday we got out and took a ferry boat across the harbour to the town. I sat in the sun in the stern and watched the ships at anchor in the mouth of the Tagus. When we stopped at the quay at the main Plaza, it seemed exactly like going ashore from a very big liner on any of my travels before the war. We went straight to a tailor and were given a complete new outfit of clothes. Then we went to an hotel where we had a last lunch together, in celebration, with the guides. The food tasted very good after our travelling and even the guides looked quite merry robbers at the table. From there we were taken in cars to the Embassy and I never saw the Poles again. I spent the night in the house of a Norwegian and revelled again in the luxury of a bath and a bed and a shave and English papers. Two nights later I went down once more to an aerodrome at night and climbed up into the fuselage by the light of the stars, but this time it was a passenger plane, and six hours later, after coming down for breakfast in Ireland by the Shannon, we arrived back in England and the long journey was at an end.

CHAPTER TWO

THE SECOND OPERATION

June 1943

After I had been back in England four days, I was called up to London and asked if I would lead the next raiding party. They apologized for asking me to go back into the field so soon, only they had no other leaders. The target we were attacking was the lock gates of the main St. Quentin canal up near the Belgian frontier. This canal carried the biggest volume of traffic of any in France and was the chief

artery of German communications between the North Sea
and the Mediterranean. Many dismantled submarines and E
boats were transported along it, apart from the other traffic.
We aimed to blow up the twin lock gates at L... and thus
flood the countryside and drain the canal completely. Like
all our operations it was ordered by the Chiefs of Staff and
co-ordinated with the strategic bombing policy of the
R.A.F.

The concept of the plan was brilliant, but the execution
would be difficult. There were many German troops in St.
Quentin itself and it was not known whether they or French
gendarmes guarded the locks. There were considerable Ack-
Ack defences and fighter aerodromes in that area, so it
looked as though the initial dropping might be sticky. The
party consisted of ten officers and I was originally given two
Halifax aircraft. If it was wanted, the R.A.F. would put in a
diversionary bombing attack against some nearby target.
When the job was completed we would escape to a rendezvous in the west of France where a bomber would land
and take us off again. C was sent on a moon ahead to make
all preliminary arrangements and do the necessary reconnaissance and report back to me by the secret wireless. He
left by a Lysander plane, which would land him in a clearing
near Paris.

After I had seen him off I went up to Norfolk for three
days leave to see the 2nd Battalion again — a pleasure
which I had promised myself through many a long night of
my travels abroad. The camp with its lines of Sherman
tanks was hidden deep in the pine woods. One afternoon I
played cricket for the battalion against some village side
and I felt young and irresponsible again in the sun, forgetting the future for those few hours; and when I left the field
I remembered the commanding officer's handshake and his
farewell: 'Good-bye now and good luck to you, and look
after yourself, Hugh, till we see you again.' I remembered
those words often during the next few months and especially on the night I left England again and set my face away

from them for the second time.

I knew I was off to France in a month and the night before I left to return to London I walked with Julian for hours through the woods, and when we came back the moonlight was flooding through the open door of my hut and I was desperately sad to leave him. When he had gone I walked again most of the night round the camp, still now with sleeping guardsmen; and I cried — as I cried the night I left the battalion for good at Warminster — because there was so much of me bound up there in that wood.

July 1943

The next month passed extremely busily in organization and preparing the equipment, most of which I had specially made in London. There were maps to be printed and rucksacks to be designed. Periodically we used to get wireless messages from C in France, reporting the progress of his arrangements, which were going a little dangerously. To practice the exact placing of the charges we used to go down at night to the Thames at Teddington or the London docks and practice the details again and again and again — usually not getting home before daylight. I would dine in my mother's flat in Chelsea and afterwards meet the others on the steps of St. Paul's and then we would all drive to the East India Docks. Sometimes there would be an air raid on overhead while we were working — sometime odd generals would come down to watch — and sometimes it would rain.

We were living at the time in a house in the country. One day my former room companion left for Yugoslavia, where he was going out to train the patriot forces. His place was taken for a time by a squadron leader just back from Cairo who had been secretary to the Air Marshall in Command in the Middle East.

We had aerial photographs taken by the R.A.F. of the St. Quentin canal and these we used to study in great detail with a special lens. It seemed fantastic to look down on that canal sleeping peacefully in the sunlight in its ignorance, while hundreds of miles away we were preparing such destruction. But modern war is ruthless and only that way can one win.

We also experimented with the different methods of dealing with the sentries and practised night sniping with silencers fitted on the Stens and luminous sights on the revolvers. The food was all specially ordered and packed in the containers to fit in the bomb-rack of the aircraft. One day we took a barge up the Grand Union Canal to study the different lock gates, and everything was restful and idyllic.

Then, when all was ready, the afternoon before we were due to leave, we were taken in cars down to Cambridgeshire. Preparing to go on such a journey is always like leaving the old world for good — growing a moustache, sending all one's uniform and private belongings home, sending my signet ring back to my mother, and then watching the English countryside flash past the car windows in the July heat for the last time.

When at the very end one got into that car to be driven out to the aerodrome with all the blinds drawn as in a hearse (lest any German agent should photograph one dressed in the clothes for France) it is like dying to the old life, and one never knew if and when one would ever return. For this time there could be only one result to our expedition, whatever the cost. When I said good-bye to my mother on the doorstep of Cranmer Court, I knew how long were the odds of my homecoming, but I did not dare to say so.

For the next four days we waited at the aerodrome as the weather was unfavourable on the other side. One afternoon C and I went into Cambridge and lay on the banks of the river and talked of our work. He never expected to last six months and had married a wife only three weeks ago, and in such circumstances one's conversation ran on odd lines. Subsequently he was to fly out on three different nights over France without being dropped for various reasons. That is a great nervous ordeal, which I was never called upon to face, as each time one climbs up into the aircraft one turns away finally from one's family and England, and it is such a shock then to return. A month later he asked for permission to come and see me off at the aerodrome. I always remember how, when I was about to take with me the lethal tablet (which one is meant to keep in one's mouth and to swallow on capture to avoid any information being tortured out of one by the Gestapo), he said that surely I would not strike my colours in that way, and I decided I never would.

The weather reports used to come through about tea-time and not till then did one know whether one would be leaving that night or not. Once we were all keyed up and ready to go — only to hear that the trip was cancelled at last, three hours before leaving. I had a lot of things on my mind all these days and I used to dread the nights for the nightmares they brought. I knew I needed to build up a reserve of sleep and used to go to bed early, but I would only awake sweating and terrified at my dreams an hour later, to find it was still daylight outside the blinds.

The fifth morning C and I sat in a cornfield against a stook sewing buttons on to some overalls of mine till midday, and we arrived back to find the whole place looking for me as the operation had just been called off. A wireless message had been received that morning to say that the trap had been sprung. Someone had talked in St.Quentin, one hundred people had been arrested and German troops were manning all the locks. Our journey under such conditions was obviously pointless, so we all drove back to London. I felt exhausted to have the tension of my mind suddenly relaxed. All my labours for the last two months were in vain; yet ten men's lives had been saved and that was no mean reprieve.

CHAPTER THREE
THE THIRD OPERATION

Preparation

July 1943

I went up to Harrogate to see my mother and mooned about in the hotel there dejectedly. I was in the depths of depression. I felt that perhaps the work was too difficult and that I would never succeed. We had been almost laughed at in Cambridgeshire for our temerity and I felt that I was wrong ever to have taken on these missions with men who were so completely English as myself. I had been offered the alternative, if I wanted it, of returning to my regiment,

However, I decided in the end to persevere with the work.

I returned to London and said I would take on the next job — to try again where I had failed before and destroy the shale oil mine and distillery plant near Le Creusot, the only one of its kind in the country working entirely for the Germans. It employed two thousand men and worked day and night, and when we finally succeeded, we destroyed the fuel and supplies of many Armoured Divisions in Russia and North Africa. This target was considered the most important target in France; that was why they wanted me to try again. I did not know whether my last attempt had alarmed the whole neighbourhood or whether the Germans had now taken over the guarding of the mine or whether I could succeed where we had once failed. It meant repeating again the whole laborious and at times mentally agonizing process with no novelty about it whatsoever. For I remembered only too well the sweat and the cold we had endured in those same hills before. The operation was planned for the August moon and D was to be dropped four days ahead.

The next three weeks were again feverishly busy. We attended a course in industrial recognition so that we should know our way about the plant in the dark and be able to identify the key pillars we were going to attack and to know the alternative targets to blow up, if the pillars were too closely watched. Most of our training was done at night and we would sleep during the daytime.

We were originally going to rehearse the whole operation against a similar mine in Scotland, which had been copied by the engineers who had built the one in France; but at the last minute the R.A.F. objected, as it would have been too dangerous to fly by night through the balloon barrage over the Firth of Forth. So we did it in two parts. The practice 'drop' we did in Gloucestershire on the darkest and windiest of nights. I just missed a fence on landing and my boots struck sparks from the barbed wire which tore my parachute to shreds; two others fell in the trees, but no one was hurt. Then we took the night train up to Edinburgh and practised the actual attack. I went in alone the night before and reconnoitred the plant, as I would soon have to in France. It was very eerie and frightening among all that hissing and moving machinery in the dark and, when after three hours I returned to the car outside, I said that the job, if it did not cost me my life, would take ten years off it. For I remembered how frightening the lights and noise of the mine had seemed, when D and I had merely watched from outside the wire last time. In London on the way back I arranged all the details of our escape through Spain.

One afternoon Jean and I walked together along the hills and then towards sunset we sat on the terrace of a café overlooking Box Hill. Jean was only twenty and his parents were still in France — that was why I only knew him under another name. I can see now so clearly that valley and the standing corn and the sun behind the hills, as I talked of our approaching journey — and of how much better it was to die young and voluntarily for a cause that was worth the martyrdom — and how Jean had not liked my conversation and said he was fond of life and hoped to live to enjoy it in its maturity. But he was wrong and I was right, for a month later he went to his death in France.

July 1943

And now in a fortnight's time, wind and weather and the moon permitting, I shall be across the seas again. Each night one listens to the droning of our bombers outward bound through the night skies, and remembers that soon now one will be a traveller with them too again. From boyhood the full moon had always attracted me strongly and would call me out to long night walks when I was still in the battalion at Fonthill Park; and now this romantic impulse had received a military foundation. We are only dropped behind the enemy lines when the moon is at its fullest, as navigation is impossible otherwise. As the throttling down of the Halifax engines warns the parachutist he is about to jump, so the steady waxing of the young July moon each night warns me of my approaching journey.

As always when faced with death, cold and premeditated, I feel a strong sense of exhilaration and goodness, and remember always the last words of Nurse Cavell the night before she faced a German firing squad: 'As I stand now before God and eternity, I realize that patriotism is not enough. I must have no hatred or bitterness towards anyone.' For it has always seemed that the conception of these expeditions embodies fully the Elizabethan qualities of daring and resource, and that same combination of love of adventure and love of one's country, which I have come lately to appreciate so well.

But times are different and we now face darker perils without the ancient consolation of public feeling and the martyr's fame. If one is caught by the Germans, one is tortured incessantly and scientifically until by pain and hunger the will is broken and that priceless information concerning the safety of other men's lives is finally extracted. In my own head lies the fatal knowledge which could send many brave men and women in France to their deaths and it is at times a terrifying responsibility. There is none of the glamour of the scaffold and the guillotine, no opportunity for the last words of Charles I standing bareheaded in the falling snow and crying that he died for the liberties of England. It is all done so secretly that the world will never know whether you faced your torturers with closed lips to the end, or whether you broke down and screamed for mercy at the first blow. And the result either way will be the same, death — shoddy and ignominious—in a civilian suit of clothes, like a rat finally hunted to exhaustion by its persecutors. Few people in England realize the shabby truth behind those stirring lines in a newspaper: 'Twelve Patriots were executed at Lille for subversive activities to the German State.'

A man must not lose the sublime vision of his ideals in the inevitable sordidness and technicalities of their mechanism among men. Too often we see only the selfishness and pettiness of the individual architects of those ideals, and forget those more transient moments of sacrifice and heroism. Things appear romantic enough in prospect and retrospect, that at the time are only monotony, and sweat, and thirst, and sickening fear.

Last night I walked in the rose garden with John and argued that the men in this organization, underneath all their cynicism and selfishness, must have high ideals. There is no other motive to warrant the running of the risks, for there is no fame or rewards or money attached to the work, and in any case death is not worth any of these. And I argued too that to defy one's torturers one would need those high ideals and only by their aid would it be possible to do so. For only then would one have sufficient strength of mind and determination to resist the pain, as the Catholic martyrs in England at the time of the persecution defied the rack and the rope. They were trained at Douay in France to redeem England, as I am being trained in England to redeem France.

And when I said that to meet death under such circumstance would be to meet it at its best, John replied: 'Yes, because then you would have really known yourself though it cost you your life to do so.' And he quoted de Musset:

'Celui qui n'a jamais souffert ne se connait pas.'

Certain it is that we poor ignorant mortals are always possessed by that curiosity to know ourselves as the Greeks recommended and we are entirely dependent on the estimation of our fellow men to hold that only mirror to our eyes.

During this last fortnight, as we had not much left to do, we used to go and harvest in the fields all day and I was happy and at peace again, listening to the drone of the tractor and helping the farmer and his daughters to bind the corn into stooks under the blazing sun; and everything was radiant. And so the time drew on to the beginning of the moon and D's departure.

(Thursday) August 12th

After an early and rather silent dinner which was to be D's last meal of his life on English soil, we left for the aerodrome. Not many words were spoken on the way; perhaps he had a presentiment of the future; perhaps he was thinking of his newly married wife and the child to come in a few months; perhaps it was only the normal burden of anticipation and the screwing up of one's nerves to face the unknown. For a lad of twenty-one, who a year before had been a private in the Belgian army, he was facing a great responsibility and a great ordeal.

We went straight to the dressing shed where D was helped into all his cumbersome flying kit and parachute harness. The R.A.F. crew of the Halifax clustered round, joking and talking in their English way to keep his spirits up. The navigator whispered to me: 'Poor devil, I pity him having to sit with all that stuff on him for four hours.'

A last look at maps and the final words of encouragement and advice and we went outside to the waiting plane. I shall never forget that picture of D, burdened down with all his kit, standing with his fair hair under the electric light of the hut, chewing furiously some American gum and making all the time such an obvious effort to present a cheerful exterior to the world of curious spectators around him. He looked that night the real picture of a Belgian patriot and martyr, the part he was in fact to play in three weeks' time.

The four engines of the great bomber were roaring in the slipstream. D was to be the only passenger in the plane that night, and indeed the only human cargo in all these twenty-three Halifaxes leaving too. He looked and must have felt very lonely, knowing, as both he and I did, that when one goes down in the moonlight into France one enters again the gates of a prison. The crew of the Halifax will be eating their breakfast back in the safety of England by dawn, but for us the future stretches away uncertain in the morning light with all its dangers and surprises that no man can foretell, except only that they will come. The first time one goes to France all is new and an adventure, but the second time one knows well the sweat and the ordeals ahead, and if there is a Hell on earth it is the crossing of the Pyrenees by night.

With a last handshake to his friends and all our wishes D clambered up into the fuselage of the bomber and the door clanged shut behind him with an awful air of finality. I knew well the thoughts of the man inside and how after that last sight of English faces and of English soil one must turn away and concentrate exclusively all one's attention on the work ahead. One dies to the old world and is eager only for the new life to begin.

We watched the plane taxi out on to the runway and then thunder down it and up into the night. Another mission had started; another page of history was being written.

I was very upset by having to witness D's departure and I could not have stood the strain much longer. It all seemed so fantastic, standing there on the aerodrome in the failing light, while above us in the sky the nightly armada droned steadily southward to the enemy coast.

We drove back to London in silence, my thoughts being always in that plane, and when I finally got home about one a.m. to my flat and kissed my mother good-night and climbed between the sheets of my comfortable bed, little did I know that at that same hour somewhere in France D had met with an accident on jumping and was hanging head downward unconscious in the trees with his parachute billowing above him in the night wind.

THE SECOND LANDING IN FRANCE

(Monday) August 16th

We left for the aerodrome in the stillness of a lovely summer's evening, while the boys playing in the village street outside paused to stare curiously at the car as it passed. Everything ended up in the usual mad last minute hurry and I remembered only the words of one of the Stonor martyrs: 'If I have courage, it is because I have not the time to think whether I have courage or no.' Under my coat I wore a white cricket shirt with the collar open for coolness and a red geranium in my button hole and once again held Henry V under my arm. I had washed and shaved before dinner and felt clean for the last time for several weeks to come. It seemed curious to be treading the very same path again as three months ago, as though it was all some nightmare illusion and this was still the first journey and I had never travelled all those thousands of miles between.

Once again out to the roaring engines on the tarmac, the slipstream tearing one's words away, the last handshake and the setting sun and the banging of the fuselage door behind. Who could have foretold that out of the six men who climbed up into the plane that night four were already marked for death and would never return?

Like Mahomet's coffin we were now suspended for the next four hours between the two worlds. We stretched ourselves out in the dark interior of the bomber which every second flew deeper over enemy territory. The door leading into the pilot's cabin was open and through the windows of the cockpit the moon stared in, illuminating everything like daylight. Its round disc swung in the window with our changing course, like the night stars behind the masts of a ship at sea. At intervals the pilot would climb and then dive down steeply with everything shuddering and vibrating so as to confuse the flak and radio-location posts beneath us. Speech was impossible in that noise. A was having a bad attack of earache again and even I found the whole journey much more unnerving than last time. Perhaps it was that now one knew the ordeal one was facing, and the price on one's head, and had lost that courage which comes from ignorance.

I lay in the dark and thought of all those people sleeping in their beds back in England and how serenely oblivious they were of the dangers we were facing. So secret are these operations that only the handful of people back in the aerodrome knew anything at all of what was happening. Yet I did not grudge them the snugness of their sheets, but only promised that, if ever I returned to England by the grace of God and lay again in a warm bed on a cold night, I would remember those who would be up and working outside at the same hour in the full moon. I thought of all those people whom I had ever befriended in my life and who I knew wished me well, and as always in danger and hardship their prayers were a great encouragement and support. And I thought too how strange it would be, if one could look into the future a few days, even a few hours ahead, and see what it held for each one of us, lying there in the darkness of the fuselage. And then again the spirit faltered and one wished to be returning home.

On the way we dropped some containers to a reception committee and it was an extraordinary experience to look down at the line of red lights and the figures running across the field, as the parachutes with their weapons and explosives went down in the moonlight into France against the time of her great uprising on that unbelievable day for which so many had been working and waiting those long years.

The hole was now uncovered and I gazed down at the fields and roads gliding beneath in the pale light of the moon with here and there the dark patches of the woods. The pilot was searching for his lights, then seeing them he banked steeply and turned for the run-in. The light opposite me flashed to red and I swung my legs into the hole. In a few seconds I should have jumped again down into that prison of Europe and the Halifax would be turning home for England. One will never forget the tension of that moment as the parachutist listens to the slowing down of the engines to stalling speed and then the light flashes to green and one is through the hole and into the rush of the slipstream, then drifting high over the earth in the peace of the moonlight. All those weeks of apprehension and the nightmares which burden one's sleeping dreams are over, and the work has begun.

In a few moments I had touched down in a field and my parachute was billowing on the ground beside me. I heard a whistle and D in a dark roll-top sweater and a beret was running across to meet me. I had seen him last four days ago on an aerodrome in Cambridgeshire and here we were met again in the middle of the night somewhere in France. How strange is life! We embraced each other warmly in the moonlight and I was desperately glad to see him again.

He told me where the package was and ran off to collect the stick. The container we found easily about seventy yards away in a hedge; the lighting system had broken, but the luminous discs helped us to find it. The rest of the party were starting to arrive by this time, and I left them to break down the container and roll up the extra two parachutes belonging to it and the package, while I walked down the hill to meet D. Neither of us could find A anywhere and after looking in the trees and whistling everywhere, I decided he must be lost, and we would therefore rely on the emergency arrangements for finding him after ninety minutes. D and I then returned together and D led the party off to some rabbit holes which he had prepared at the bottom of a wooded dell. The ground was hard as rock, there having been no rain for the last month, and it would have been quite impossible to bury anything without D's previous reconnaissance. Here we all stripped and I left R in command of the digging operations while D and I went off to look for A. There was a plane which kept circling round the neighbourhood and I warned R to be extremely careful not to flash torches. It was pitch dark where he was digging and this was not easy.

Certain incidents of the next few days have sunk deep in my memory — an hour after landing that first glimpse through the trees of the village of Barnay again, as we walked through the same fields in France as three months ago and how the same cattle were browsing there. Here we were four hundred miles behind the enemy lines and how quiet the houses lay in the moonlight. How the rain pelted down on us in the woods one night with no cover, until we were all shivering and S was expecting a recurrence of his malaria and my own fingers were white and wrinkled with the cold like parchment; and how the hours seemed to pass interminably to the dawn, while in the distance we could hear the rumbling of the mine which soon we were to destroy.

I walked off to the rendezvous I had previously arranged in the event of anyone still being lost after ninety minutes. We arrived to find A waiting for us, at which I was very impressed. The place was over a mile from the dropping point, through thick woods and not at all easy to find at night. He told me he had walked on the North Star, and I was very relieved to see him. I had been afraid he might have fallen in the trees and been knocked out and his parachute might have given the alarm at daylight. Though he had landed quite close to the stick, he was probably the wrong side of a hedge and it was very difficult country to contact in — as I know to my own cost from the last operation.

When we returned the digging was finished, and collect-
ing the cells we moved off to the first hide-out, which D
had chosen about a mile and a half from the dropping
point. D and I carried the package, slung between us on a
pole rather in the style of Indian tiger hunters. We left the
party hidden in a thicket, and he and I walked back again
to collect his blanket, rucksack and torches which he had
left on the side of the dropping field. It was nearly dawn
and I felt that luck had been well with us so far and everything had gone according to plan. On the way back D told
me of his own adventures up to date.

Both he and the package had landed in the trees and he
had been knocked unconscious immediately. He had come
to four hours later at dawn, to find himself hanging head
downwards and his head banging against a branch in the
wind. His parachute was caught up above him. Of the package, he had no idea.

He managed to cut himself down and buried his parachute. All that day he looked for the package but could find
no trace of it anywhere; it was not finally found till two days
later. As he had a bad headache and had no food or reception equipment, he had no alternative but to go off that
night to the farm where he had stayed on the last operation.
This had not been in my plan at all, owing to the danger to
security, but circumstances left him no choice. When he
walked into the farmyard that night the son met him and
said, 'I thought it was you when I heard the plane circling
last night'. D managed to laugh that one away and told
them that he was in charge of a party of British airmen who
were hiding in the woods and that the plane had dropped a
package of food for them. This fitted in with his previous
story as an R.A.F. pilot escaping after being shot down in
May. He had gone to Paris and then been sent south again
by the organization to contact a second lot of escaping airmen three months later. The farmer was delighted to see
him anyway and gave him all help and food. He also told D
that the Germans had been searching the local farms for

some men who were supposed to have baled out of a British plane. Whether D had been seen dropping by the German observation post across the valley (which was easily in view of the field) or whether the Germans were looking for the crew of a bomber, which I subsequently learnt had been shot down about forty miles away, we never discovered. But in any case I decided to move carefully.

The son had then returned with D the next day and after searching the woods all afternoon he found the package for him and they brought it back to the farm. Everyone was a little mystified when the torches were unpacked, but D explained how they were used for map reading. The wireless receiving set D rigged up secretly in a corner of the barn and no one ever saw it. The set worked perfectly and D picked up the B.B.C. message two nights later.

His accident on landing and the loss of the package left him very short of time, and he was only able to go down one afternoon and have a quick look at the wood we had used last time as the final hide-out before the attack. This was now thickly overgrown and not disturbed by woodcutters; he decided to use it again as the last base. The charges were still there under the earth, though the strikers in the time pencils had all come down. The binoculars he brought back and gave to the farm. He reconnoitred a new and much better route down from the dropping point through the woods nearly all the way. This he signposted with the small luminous discs which looked like glow-worms in the dark. He walked along the road past the factory and saw at once that the approach from the west was impossible. He found out by discreet conversation at the farm that there were no German guards at Les Telots, that the plant was still working hard, that it employed about two thousand men and that in Autun there were no German troops, but only an officer cadet school and the gendarmerie. Otherwise everything was peaceful in the neighbourhood.

He then prepared the holes, and put out the lights on the stick's dropping ground when he heard the B.B.C. message,

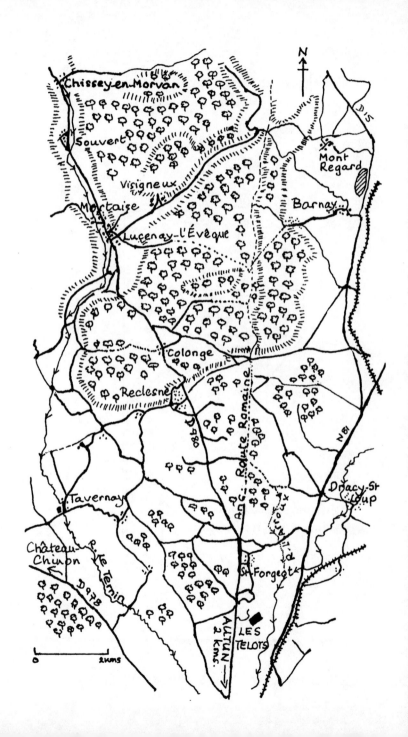

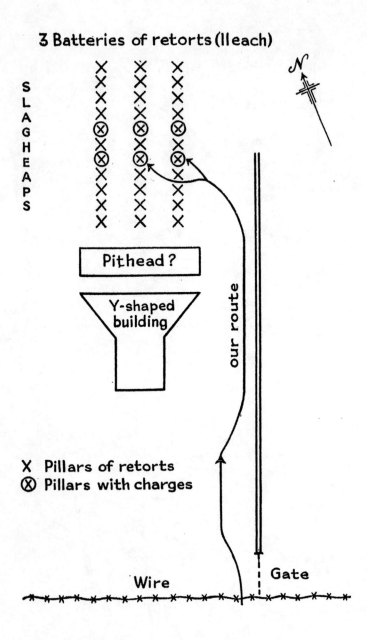

and waited with a chicken, a dozen eggs and a gourd full of wine and three bottles of water for our arrival. Owing to the drought water was very scarce. All the streams were dried up and even the farms were very short. He was dozing in a blanket under the hedge when he heard the plane a quarter of an hour early. After getting the recognition signal, he flashed his white torch in the centre of the field and used that as a guide to the red lights as he was afraid of their being masked by the trees. When the aircraft banked for the run-in, he ran back to the red torches and indicated the line in the usual manner.

PREPARATION AND RECONNAISSANCE

The rest of the day passed pleasantly enough. We broke down the package and the cells and distributed the food and charges. Each man carried his share in his own rucksack and was completely self-contained. The cells we hid under some very thick bushes, it being impossible to dig. The chicken and wine were much appreciated. I posted sentries on the nearest path till midday and then I arranged merely that one man should always be awake where we were lying. The morning passed quickly enough with chess and cards. D and G (wearing corduroys) went back to the farm in the afternoon for more water. This was necessary owing to the drought and I had planned originally for S and G to hide up in the farm after the attack and wanted one of them to know the route back. G was introduced as one of the airmen hiding in the woods and D tore a ten franc note in half and gave a part each to the farmer and G, and arranged the passwords in case things went wrong later and someone else needed to visit the farm. The farm was about one and a half hours walk away through the woods and they were not back until late in the afternoon. We all got some welcome sleep.

On the night of August 17th-18th (Tuesday and Wednesday) S and I, as previously planned, left the party and set off for the wood which D had chosen for the last hide-out. We each carried a rucksack with our food and charges and both of us wore corduroys. The same night D and G buried the escaping food and clothes belonging to A and G at a convenient cross-track, which they would pass on their way back to the farm after the attack. In this way we slightly lessened the loads which had to be carried down to the final wood. D afterwards returned again to the farm to collect water, as the weather was extremely hot.

S and I crossed the main road at the bottom of the woods without incident before the moon rose. At two points on the route we had to pass by farms but nobody was awake. On the last part of the journey I misunderstood D's directions and we missed a certain track junction with the result that morning found us lost in the wrong wood and we narrowly escaped being seen by a man ploughing in the next field. Here we waited all the day, and in the afternoon, as there was no one working in the heat, I went off to pick up my bearings. I soon found the right wood and filled the water bottles. I also chose the exact spot in the wood where the cover was thickest and it was farthest away from any paths. It is absolutely essential to do this previously by daylight, as it is impossible to arrive in the dark and then pick a suitable hide-out. I then returned to S at about six p.m.

That night S and I moved up to the final wood, and I decided it was too late to make a full reconnaissance of the target that night as we had originally planned. I therefore used the hours of darkness to reconnoitre only the first part of the route up to the second bridge, which was the most difficult and where we had been stopped on the last operation.

On our return at about three a.m., I met D, who had just arrived down with the main party. They had had an uneventful journey and covered the most dangerous part between the farms before the moon rose. I then took them to the exact spot in the wood I had chosen for the hide-out, and we all waited there till daylight. G's cough was very bad again with the cold.

All that day passed quietly enough with cards and reading.

We were very fortunate throughout the operation with the weather. In the afternoon heat I took the water bottles down and filled them in a stream. The water was fairly thick, but the only available, and I never knew anyone suffering from drinking the dirty water.

At nightfall S and I set out to reconnoitre the factory. I took D and A also on the first part up to the second bridge, so that they could memorize the route too and explain it to the others. At the bridge we left them and went on alone. S carried the wirecutters and a pair of corduroys for me, in case I was detained inside the factory and we had to make the return journey after daybreak. We moved as fast as possible as I wanted to cross the wire before the moon rose. At the last hedge I left S and went on alone.

I first tried a new approach into the factory and walked across the open levelled ground to the south-west of the refinery till I met the wire. I was kneeling down examining the thickness of the mesh, when I hear a crunch of gravel behind me and two men bicycled past not ten yards away on a path I had not noticed. I did not hear them till they were on me and I was lucky not to be seen. Then for the next fifteen minutes there was a stream of workmen along the same path, some on foot and some on bicycles. It was getting lighter with the rising moon and there was no cover whatsoever as the ground was quite flat, so I lay on my face and hoped their lights would not happen to fall on me. I realized that it must be the time when the shifts were changed over and all the workmen had to pass along the path to enter by the gate which was just around the corner. I knew that if I was still there when the moon had risen I could not avoid being noticed, so taking advantage in a momentary break in the traffic, I got up and walked back across the levelled ground to S.

I was rather glad to see him again and waited there a few moments to get my breath back. We then went down the hedge to where the bridge crossed the river and here I left S again with instructions to observe the traffic on the bridge, while I went on to try the gate we had discovered on the last operation. I reached it all right, and hearing no noise from the sentry-box beside it, walked up the bank and climbed over the wire by the gate. For a man without charges this was comparatively easy.

I then worked my way over towards the slag-heaps and followed them up into the factory. I was crawling about all among pools of slag-water and fell in once up to my knees in the slime and had great difficulty in extricating my gym shoes. The smell of the shale remained on my overalls for some days afterwards.

I passed a hut that housed the water pump, which made a lot of noise but had nobody inside it, and eventually arrived alongside the Y-shaped building which appeared to be a fresh shale dump. Trucks were arriving all the time along an overhead cable and tipping shale out on an open heap which went the whole length of the building. There were three or four workmen supervising the machinery.

By this time the moon had come up behind the slag-heaps. It was still nearly full and it lit up everything like day; I was lying behind some old pipes and saw that I could now get no further past the Y building without being seen, as this also had its own lights which shone at the completely open side, the building being nothing but an iron roof.

I could not think what to do next, and it was only the fact that I realized I was still no nearer knowing anything about the retorts, that decided me to push on at all costs. So I then turned left and climbed up the first slag-heap. By this means I kept in shadow from the moon and the going was fairly easy. When I reached the shaft and rails for the trucks I sat down and took stock of the situation.

I was now opposite the near end of the retorts and about level with the top. There were many more men than I ever expected to find working. I counted four men who appeared at different times on the top of the retorts at eye-level; underneath, where the men were emptying the hoppers, there was a lot of activity. Between the Y building and the retorts there was another tall building, which was the noisiest of the lot and where I noticed several men walking underneath and also up and down an iron staircase which ran up the outside. I wondered if this could be the head of the mine, as underneath the slag-heap where I was sitting the ground rumbled incessantly. I am sure the mine was very near.

I did not like to stay there long as the moon was still rising and I was afraid of being spotted by the men on the top of the retorts, who periodically came up for some air and leant against the railings opposite me. But I still knew nothing about the vital fact as to whether the pillars of the retorts were made of concrete or not.

So after a few minutes I walked down the truck railway which of course led me to the bottom of the retorts. The railway on this slag-heap was not being used, though the control cabin at the bottom was lit up inside with the door open and there were three trucks full of burnt shale standing on the rails. I crawled past the cabin and ended up at the end pillar of the retorts. The men were emptying the hoppers about five pillars up where the trucks all came out on this side. They were emptied into some cooling apparatus, for each time there was a lot of hissing and clouds of steam. There was never an interval of more than two minutes between the emptying of the trucks.

When I touched the last, an end pillar, I was horrified to see that its surface was white and fairly smooth. It certainly was not a brick surface and I at once jumped to the conclusion that it was concrete. My feelings can best be imagined. Thinking that the pillars were of concrete and therefore unassailable, I retired up my slag-heap again to consider the situation.

I knew I must find an alternative target or else retreat for good and waste the whole value of my reconnaissance so far. When, three nights later, we did attack the middle pillars, it was quite obvious to everybody that they were built of brick. I can only presume therefore that the outside surface of the end pillar, which was all that I could get near enough to that night, was plaster cast for some reason, as it was a completely different colour and texture from the middle ones.

To see the other side of the factory better I crossed over to the second slag-heap, which was not being used. From here in the moonlight I could see the lay-out of the whole plant with the road on the far side. This slag-heap looked enormous in the night and the top of it towered above me where there was a hut and a red light. It was much bigger than the ones in Scotland and had paths and disused huts along the side.

Below me near the road was a large building with white smoke coming out incessantly which I took to be the boiler house. The exhaustors it was impossible to trace at that height, even with night glasses, and in any case they would have been too near the front entrance. I ruled them out as a possibility right away. The winding gear of the mine I could never have found either; which left only the conveyor.

So I descended the slag-heap again and on my withdrawal took a look at the conveyor in the distance. This also had men working on the top where it ran into the retorts and at the bottom the supports were very close to the main railway to the station. Two trains had passed in and out since I entered the factory. I had now been in about three hours and it was nearly two o'clock in the morning. I decided to go home.

I had one or two lucky escapes again on my way back to the wire, as I discovered that there was a worker's restroom in a hollow fifty yards from the gate I had entered by. This had not been in use then at eleven p.m., but I could now hear voices inside and saw the lights. As the gate was the only exit I knew I decided to climb it again and was halfway over it when three men walked by to the refreshment room. I was certain they must have seen me in the full moonlight as they stopped and talked for a moment — but as always at night one imagines the worst automatically and magnifies the dangers, for there was no alarm and no pursuit.

However, I had dropped down again inside the wire and decided to leave that neighbourhood as quickly as possible. I followed along the wire to where it ran up the side of the slag-heap and by scrambling halfway up it again I reached the end of the wire where it just petered out. I passed around it, down the far side, along the river under the two bridges and found S trying to get some sleep under the hedge. He told me that, shortly after I left, a watchman (whom D and I saw on that same bridge on the last operation) had stood about on the bridge when the trains were running across into the factory and he had only just gone way.

On the way home we inspected the hedge where I had left the two sets of charges on the last operation. The charges were still there but the rucksack was gone. It definitely had not rolled away as the charges were fairly scattered about.— but I expect there was really some simple explanation for the curiosity. On the way back from the factory we lost ourselves (just as D and I had done last time). Finding the route back was very tricky, as the streams and rivers branched everywhere and one had to memorize between which farms one had to pass. We came out on the main road to the north of the factory, but as we had still two hours of moonlight left we went back again and memorized in great detail the exact route. I was very afraid that in the excitement and confusion after the attack I would not find the right way back across the fields (as did in fact happen in the thick mist).

We arrived back in the woods about five a.m. to find the others sleeping hard.

At daylight we had some food and a hot drink and I gave the others an account of the preceding night. After talking with G, who had worked in the building trade, it appeared that the surface of the pillar might have been rough cast and not concrete. It was obviously impossible anyway to attack the retorts without being seen. I also decided that I would not take six men into the factory under the conditions of full moonlight that I had encountered; that would have been suicidal. With charges they could never have climbed over the wire in any case.

The situation looked rather depressing, but I decided to wait for three nights anyhow, as by that time the moon would not have risen before one a.m. The weather, which had been perfect for a month, showed no signs of breaking. Exactly what target we would attack I had not decided.

We could not stay in the woods without more food, so that night D and A and I walked back to the farm. The distance must have been over eight miles as it took us three hours. We took an empty rucksack each for the food and D took all his own clothes with him in case I decided to send him back to Paris direct. I took A with us in order that there should be one man in each pair who knew the way to the farm in case of emergency. R I left in command of the party.

We had an uneventful journey back and we were all getting to know the countryside fairly well by this time — at least by night. We re-christened the Ancient Route Romaine the Route Anglaise as it was the main artery of our communications and each night some of us had been along it, either southward with charges or northward in search of food.

(Friday and Saturday) August 20th-21st

We arrived at the farm about two a.m. A slept in the barn and D and I slept in the spare room in an enormous wooden bed. This was civilization indeed. Here we slept till daybreak when the farmer came in from next door and got a pleasant surprise to find us back again. We had an excellent breakfast which made the long walk almost worthwhile.

This was the farm where D had stayed on the last operation and for two nights before this one. We called it Parachute Farm as it was littered with our equipment. The two sons wore our blue overalls from last time; meals were eaten with the clasp knives we had given them; the binoculars were on the mantelpiece; in the cellar there were two thirty-twos; we slept under the Army blankets which D had given them after the last operation; the reception torches provided the illumination for the evening meal and the farmer used an old spine-pad as a seat for his plough. It was a real home and we were treated royally.

I spent the day talking with the farmer generally. By this time everyone had a fairly shrewd idea of what we were after in the neighbourhood, and he seemed to think there was quite an army of us hiding up in the woods. By the afternoon, with the assistance of one of his friends who knew a workman in the factory, I had discovered that there were definitely no armed guards at Les Telots. This was of vital importance and it was only on the assurance of this information that I decided to attack the target in the way we did.

In the evening D, having completed his role, caught the bus for Paris, where he warned the organization of our probable arrival. That night A and I walked back to the wood again with food for the others. I also arranged with the farmer that after the attack we would return and hide up in the woods near the farm until the excitement died down. He on his part offered to feed us indefinitely and help us in every way with pressing clothes and giving us all the local information about trains. I fixed a rendezvous by a fountain with his son when we left, and they all turned out to wish us the best of luck.

(Saturday and Sunday) August 21st-22nd

A and I returned to the others at one a.m. It was pouring with rain and a vile night generally. Sleep was out of the question and everybody sat and shivered till daylight. R was afraid of a recurrence of malaria, but fortunately this did not happen. In the morning the others wanted to go to a farm nearby and get their clothes dried, but I decided this was only taking unnecessary risks. It continued to rain on and off all day.

THE ATTACK

As the moon would not rise before one a.m., I decided to attack that night wet or fine. In the afternoon A and S made up the charges and each man packed his own into his small pack. I burnt the aerial photographs. The rucksacks, with all the clothes and food we did not need that night, we packed and left in order by the edge of the path. I marked them by a luminous disc so we should find them quickly again on our return in the dark.

My plan for the night was this. Owing to the number of men working, it was impossible to do the job silently. As there were no armed guards there and as six men suddenly appearing in the middle of the night would look like sixty, I decided to hold the workers up while we put the charges on and to rely on our bluff not being called. Everybody would carry his own charges up to the wire and there I and S would give ours to A and R, who would thus place a double set of charges each, as they were the most efficient pair at charge placing and had practised together in England. B and G would work as a pair and place a single set each. S and I would be left free to hold the workmen up. S and I took two pistols each to present a more ferocious appearance.

Each man was to wear a mask in case of recognition later.

No English was to to be spoken at all and we decided to announce ourselves under the ambiguous title of 'les forces de la liberté'. My French being very imperfect, S and I between us wrote out the following speech for the workmen and after frequent rehearsals I could repeat it without prompting by the evening:

Ne bougez pas. Ne parlez pas. Nous avons un travail a faire. Il faut nous aider. Silence!

Ecoutez. Nous sommes les force de la liberté. L'usine va sauter. Nous sommes vos amis. L'Allemand c'est notre ennemi commun. Il faut nous aider.

L'usine va sauter en dix minutes. Ceux-ci sont des charges. C'est dynamite. Ne touchez pas. Danger de mort. Il faut maintenant aller avertir tous vos camarades et partir vite loin d'ici. Vous avez assez de temps et n'oubliez pas les ouvriers là-haut. Nous sommes venus ici pour battre les allemands, pas pour toucher les français. Entrainez toutes les efforts de la gen-

*darmerie de nous suivre. Gardez votre foi. L'heure de la libéra-
tion est proche.*

The charges were made up with ten-minute time pencils, as I dared not leave them with a longer delay for fear someone would move them, and we relied on the general confusion to make our escape. The pencils were only to be pressed when all were ready, on a pre-arranged signal. We carried both the wirecutters. By the evening there was a thick mist, and we could not have been luckier in the weather. After making sure that nothing was left lying about and all the unwanted rubbish burnt, we set out at dusk about nine-thirty p.m.

We crossed the main road by the second bridge without incident, just before a car passed, and continued up along the river. The mist was dense and one could barely see twenty yards. I stopped frequently to check the way back, and nearer the factory we left three luminous disks at different points to signpost our return. In fact we lost the way returning — even with these precautions; and the luminous discs, though not noticeable in the daytime, were probably found in the end by the Germans and given to the bloodhounds.

We then all passed through the wire and approached without being seen to about four hundred yards of the retorts. Here I left them and went on again to check up on my bearings for the last time. I returned ten minutes later and told them the last details — that the retorts were definitely of brick, the exact shape of the pillars and that, if they were sensible and kept their heads, the job would be easy. We then got up and walked openly up the railway line in pairs. We passed a dining room with an open door where there were a lot of workmen having a meal. The time was about twelve-thirty a.m.

I stopped once to let a man with a lantern go by and then walked on up to the pillars. The first one I touched with my hand, and B and G started putting the rope round and the charges on, while the other two and S branched in and started to work on the parallel pillars in the centre. I was expecting trouble and had my pistols out (one of them we had borrowed from the farm and it was rusted up terribly and would have probably exploded if fired).

There was a man sitting asleep against B's pillar, who soon woke up, and there were two other men who came up to see what was happening. I pushed a pistol into the chest of the first man and started off on the first part of my speech. When I said the factory was going to blow up, the men nodded their heads as though it was a matter of course (we subsequently learnt that they first thought we were Germans warning them to take shelter against an Allied air raid). When I said 'Nous sommes vos amis. L'Allemand, c'est notre ennemi commun. Il faut nous aider', everyone appeared only too enthusiastic and they said they had been expecting us for a long time. When I came to the phrase about 'les forces de la liberté' they started clapping us on the back.

S meanwhile was speaking on the other side of the retorts and we had gathered quite a group round us. I caught one man trying to slink away in the shadows and forced him back. We had to be very careful of this as otherwise I knew the alarm might be given while we were still working. One of the men asked permission to go home, as the factory was finished, but I told him he must wait a few minutes. They asked me of course if they would be out of work now, and I could only say that they might be needed for the repairs.

During this time I had to keep on hopping back to B and G to ensure they were not attacked whilst they were working. All the charges were on within about eight minutes and R and A must have worked at tremendous speed, as they had their double charges on at about the same time as the first two. It was only possible because they had practised the drill repeatedly before. The time pencils were then pressed together.

I went back and told the workmen not to move the charges. 'C'est dynamite. Danger de mort.' I said they would go off in ten minutes. I told them we had come here to defeat the Germans and not to kill Frenchmen, and that they must warn all their friends at once and get everybody right away from the retorts immediately. I sent a man upstairs to get the men down from the top of the retort and S did the same. We could not have done more to prevent loss of life and I was particularly insistent that everything should be done to save the men. Again this was only possible due to the rather unorthodox method of our attack.

We told them finally to hinder all the efforts of the gendarmerie to track us down, and not to lose heart, as the Allies would come soon. Everybody was most enthusiastic and S, finding himself among Frenchmen, looked happier than I had ever seen him and I am sure that to him those few minutes under the retorts were worth the consequences. B had dropped a split pin and a workman shone his lantern to help him find it. The small packs were hung on the rope alongside the charges so that they would be destroyed too.

The charges I knew would be going off soon, so the six of us vanished again into the night. There was no pursuit but a certain amount of general confusion. We were about two fields away from the wire when the first charge went off eighteen minutes from the time of pressing the pencils. In the thick night it was difficult to see clearly, but a ball of fire sailed up into the air from the top of the retorts. The five others all went off close together within the next eight minutes, the last charge being the weakest of the six. It was almost impossible to observe the results as I was in a hurry to cross the bridges and the two main roads before the police. As I feared, I lost the route in the mist, and, following the main river, we came out on the main road some way to the east of the right place.

We ran along the road through a small village and eventually back to the wood. We collected the rucksacks and set off at the fastest walking pace possible along the Roman road. We crossed the second main road between the houses and up into the woods. Here we rested a bit. All was quiet. R's foot was hurting and I knew we would never make the farm that night. We arrived back at our first hide-out of all at five a.m. S and G collected their clothes from the cross track. I left there a bottle of wine on the way down there three nights before, so we were not too badly off, though very thirsty.

All that day passed quickly and I thought that everyone would escape safely. It was impossible to walk on to the farm during the day as that would only endanger the security of the farmer.

THE PURSUIT AND ESCAPE TO PARIS

We were lying up under the trees in the peace of the evening. It looked as though all our dangers were over and in a few moments, when the sun set, we would start out on the last stage of our escape to the farm. There had been a strange quietness about the woods all day, yet I knew that after the audacity of our attack in the mine the night before someone would have to swing for it.

Suddenly a dog howled in the village of Barnay half a mile beneath us in the valley. We could just see the roofs of the houses through the green leaves. Someone said, 'Bloodhounds', and we all laughed, but the next moment they all began to bay together and there were sounds of organized activity. I knew we were in for it then. It was just getting dark under the trees and England seemed very far away.

When the silence was first broken by the baying of those bloodhounds I remember well how I was suddenly sick with fear; my limbs felt paralysed and I did not trust to the steadiness of my voice to speak. It had been easy to talk of the attractions of defiance and martyrdom back in England, but now to find oneself surrounded in the woods with night coming down and to be hunted remorselessly by one's fellow men seemed terrifying and inhuman. I realized in that moment how dearly one clings to life in the last struggle —

instinctively against all reason. The bloodhounds had obviously got our scent, otherwise they would not have started to track us at that spot in all those forests, nor would they have begun as night was falling. I knew there would be no escape.

At first we sat and listened to that intermittent howling of the dogs, one minute silent and then the next all speaking together like a pack. They seemed at first to be going away from us to the east and I thought we would wait till it was completely dark, but then we suddenly heard them again coming towards us, much nearer now in the same part of the woods as we were. I visualised how at any moment men with lanterns following the hounds on the leash would burst into the clearing where we lay, and then would follow the last desperate exchange of shots. Another band of 'Communist terrorists' would have been annihilated with all the accompanying ignominy and violence. To be tracked down like criminals and shot in a sweaty suit of clothes would not be a very glorious end. I had no wish to flee farther but would have preferred to stand and face our pursuers with what dignity was possible in the sordid circumstances.

But the others were for continuing as long as possible, so I led them out of the clearing on to the forest paths. We made an awful noise on the crackling leaves in our hurry. Once or twice I stopped to listen, as I thought I heard voices ahead and expected to run into another patrol. If they were searching the woods for us, they had presumably put a cordon round them

We walked fast in the darkness and after an hour I led them out on to the main road. By now we had left the sound of the dogs behind and all was once more silent. I spread the map out on the ground and by the shaded light of a torch showed the others exactly where we were, and gave them the final instructions to split up into pairs. Below us on the road there were some cottages with a light flashing and the noise of a motor-car engine — there was clearly no time to lose. Then we shook hands and parted and I never saw them again. Jean, who was only twenty, implored me to let him stay with me till we reached a river, but I could not. I told them all that, if we were caught, as now seemed certain, it had all been worth while whatever the cost. Then B and I left the shadow of the trees and struck out alone across the fields.

We could not have been in a more desperate position, yet nevertheless I felt a great sense of relief at having at last shed my responsibility for the others and at having now only our two lives to try and save. I had left my boots behind me in the clearing in our hurry and had only the pair of Army gym shoes I was wearing to get to Paris in. We had only a little food and no water. B neither spoke nor understood one word of French and my own accent was appalling. The bloodhounds could not be far behind. We were beggars now in reality and were throwing ourselves with complete abandon on the mercy of the world.

After walking a little farther we came out on another road and kept on it for the rest of the night. This was dangerous, but the countryside was so thick that we could not cross it except by roads and our scent would be harder to follow.

Presently we passed right through the centre of a small village. It was about eleven p.m. and there were still lights in the houses. We tried to get some water out of a well, but as we approached it a dog barked in the garden so we went on. At another place I tried to find a trough, but I stumbled against a pile of timber in the yard and I heard voices stop inside the room and a man fumbled at the door. So again we retraced our steps quickly and went on. The countryside was of course by this time deserted, it being long after curfew. Farther on we came to another village and I was perplexed at the cross roads as to which was our way. It was very hard to read a map in the moonlight. I remember there was a tall church and some poplars on the side of the road.

I eventually selected one of the roads, and a mile along it at the edge of the village we came to another cottage, whose lighted windows shone out across our way. There is no black-out in the country in France at all. Through the glass I could see a young woman in the kitchen — and she seemed alone. So I knocked on the door and said we were thirsty and could she give us to drink. After a moments hesitation she said, yes, and while we waited she heated some coffee. She kept glancing at us curiously and said we were out very late, and I said we were woodcutters going home. B of course never opened his mouth all the time.

Outside in the yard two men were loading hay on to a cart by the light of a lantern. As she seemed friendly, I put my back against the door and said outright we were Englishmen and could we have some water to shave. For I knew our beards would betray us in the daylight tomorrow. She stood stock still with the shock of my words and then a great look of fear and pity came into her eyes. She said she would like to help us, but it was not her house and she was not certain of the two men outside. Just at this moment the door opened and they came in; so finishing our coffee I said we understood perfectly and went out.

It seemed hard to leave the warmth of the kitchen for the dark road again, but we had far to go and there could be no loitering, nor could we ever return this way a second time. We walked on for another hour checking the map often and listening for sounds of any pursuit. I looked at the sky, but it was crystal clear and held no hope of rain to obliterate our scent. The road now led down into a dark valley, with trees on either side which obscured the moon. Presently we came to a stream on the edge of the village of Mortaise.[1] Here we stopped and shaved in the moonlight. We seemed incongruous standing there by the deserted river with houses a few yards away in the middle of the night. B asked me if shaving was really necessary, but I assured him it was advisable for his life and was not merely the tradition of a guardsman.

This took about twenty minutes and then we climbed back

---

[1] This seems incorrect: it was probably a village further north.

on the main Route Nationale and followed it for a short way through the village. I was nervous lest it should be patrolled, but all was silent as the grave. We soon turned off it and came to a bridge over a larger river. Here I wanted to spend some time and wade up it and so try and break the scent in the waters, but the banks were steep and B thought it was quite unnecessary as there seemed to be no pursuit. I foolishly ignored my instinct and gave in to him and we went on.

We went on for another two hours and as it was growing light in the east we came to the outskirts of Lucenay l'Evêque. This was quite a big town with several streets. We continued on into the town till our footsteps woke up a farm dog which began to bark. Once aroused they would bark all night and, though I had already ignored them several times earlier on, it seemed unnecessarily foolhardy to continue through the town on account of the lateness of the hour. The farmers would be getting up soon. So I turned off the road and went in through a gate into someone's back garden. At the other end was another fence with wire on the top and this was hard to climb over silently. I tried it in several places and had already made quite a lot of noise. The first dog was still barking and I began to feel desperate again, as any moment the owner might come out and we would have found it hard to explain what we were doing there in his garden. While I had my back to the street and we were both in the shadow of the wall, suddenly three men tore past on bicycles. They had no lights and were going flat out. They were obviously gendarmes who had gone in front of the bloodhounds to cut us off; no one else would have been out and without lights at such an hour. Had we not turned off that road by chance and been in the cover of the garden, we would have been caught by them for certain, as there is no cover in a street. It was a lucky escape, but it gave me an unpleasant suspicion that we had been followed all through the night. If that was the case, with daylight approaching our position was perilous.

We climbed over the fence at last and made our way

across some marshy land and up a hill on the edge of the town. Here we found some gorse and blackberry bushes and, as I decided we would only be seen by farmers if we continued walking, we threw ourselves down and rested. We had been walking fast without a stop all night on the hard road in gym shoes and B was feeling very tired. It was just getting light. We lay down on our coats and fell asleep. The time was about five-thirty a.m.

At six o'clock we were woken by the sound of dogs in the town. We immediately recognized the high-pitched yelping of the bloodhounds which, once heard, could never be forgotten. It sounded as though they were coming along the road and had not yet reached the point where we turned off into the garden. We had obviously been tracked all night and they were gaining on us. To hear the dogs speaking to our scent again seemed terribly remorseless and inhuman.

Once more I was for staying where we were and meeting our fate, but B seemed to have a much stronger will to survive and was all for continuing until we were caught. So we collected our things and walked over the crest of the hill. I was making west as that was where the forests lay. On the top we were held up in some thick brambles through which it took us some minutes to find a way. From there one got a good view of the countryside around and the farms still sleeping in the broad daylight. Behind us we heard the continued yelping. It was about seven-thirty.

We followed a track down the other side and crossed the main road at the bottom between two houses. There were still no signs of life except for the smoke rising from the chimneys. We followed a sunken lane which led down beneath the level of the road. Two minutes after crossing the road we heard the noise of an engine, and watched from our cover a large bus drive along and put out grey uniformed figures at all the bends. With a curious feeling of detachment we watched the organization of the German cordon to catch us. We had only slipped through it by those two minutes and, had we hesitated any longer among the blackberry bushes or been delayed by the brambles for just that extra fraction of time, we would have arrived at the main road two late and never crossed it and been caught in the net. Our luck was nearly miraculous.

We continued up the other side of the valley till we reached the cover of the woods, taking care to keep in the shadow. Even so I felt the cynosure of all eyes going up that hill, for I knew that the troops on the road might easily have field-glasses. The wood once reached was thick and had several paths and we continued along them, taking our direction from the sun. From time to time we heard the noise of more dogs and shouting above and in front of us in the same woods. It looked as though the Germans were searching all that area and casting the net wide. We seemed to have stirred up a real hornet's nest.

Sometimes the sounds were so close that I expected to see figures suddenly emerge at the bend in the path. At each track junction we chose the quietest of the alternatives and trusted in God. Presently we came out half-way down on the edge of a clearing and looked down at the valley below. Through the trees we could see the soldiers standing in pairs in the shade by the side of the road beneath us. It was a typical August morning, very hot and still.

As our position seemed desperate and we had been going a long time without anything to eat, I stopped and we opened our tin of bully beef. It seemed a pity not to have it before the Germans did, and we might soon need its sustenance. We also had a drink out of the water bottle. Then we smartened ourselves up as much as possible in case we should have to walk along the roads as the last bluff. I remember that when I took out my mirror the picture of the Little Flower[1] fell out too, and I told B that we were in such a hole that only she could get us out of it.

Yet all hope of escaping seemed gone completely. We had led them a good dance and now it only behoved us to die with dignity. Our mission in France had been accomplished;

[1] St. Thérèse of Lisieux, patron saint of soldiers.

in a few minutes we would pay the price which thousands had already paid. I remember so clearly as we sat on that hillside in the patch of sunlight thinking that we had seen the end of the story. It seemed only a pity that we would never escape to that welcome in Paris which I had enjoyed so much on my last journey, and that the tale of our doings would remain for ever unknown. By now I had long ago recovered my composure after that first moment of panic the night before; such things as executions seemed very out of place on such a delightful day.

However, we continued walking and kept on through the woods until noon. We had various fantastic theories of how to break our scent, but I am sure none of them worked, for we were only amateurs at the game. At one point we saw a young man working in a field. We approached him under cover of the trees and then I whistled him over to us in the shadow. He looked surprised at seeing anybody else about, but, after a quick look round, he came over and asked me what I wanted. He was about seventeen.

I told him outright we were Englishmen and asked him to help us. Would he give us either pepper to throw on our trail, or give me his sabots so that I could change my gym shoes to break the scent? B, having his boots too, had already changed into them. The boy seemed very sceptical of us, as though he did not believe our tale of bloodhounds. I told him he would soon see in an hour's time when they passed that way. I pointed out that it was his sabots or our lives, but he only laughed. He would never be able to get another pair and his father would be furious. He advised us to keep on walking and directed us along the best paths. He also mentioned a cottage where we might get some pepper. So I ended our argument and we went on. He refused all money and when I asked him, was he for the Germans or for us, he said he was naturally for us. He gave us the impression, like the others later, that they were the amused spectators of some game or else that we were suffering from some hallucination in hearing all these Germans in the woods. I could hardly blame him, for what were Englishmen doing in the middle of France in the broad daylight? And it did seem mad to talk of bloodhounds in the stillness of such a morning.

The paths now became overgrown with brambles and the going was extremely exhausting and slow. The sun was overhead, and we were thirsty. We stopped and had a drink. I wanted to put some water into the empty bully-beef tin and leave it in the middle of the path with a ten franc note and this message to our pursuers: 'Give the dog a drink and buy one yourself. Isn't it hot walking?' Only I was afraid of leaving them any fresh bearer of our scent, and it would also have confirmed to the Germans that we were English. In any case no one would have believed us afterwards.

As we walked along the crest of the woods, we had the curious experience of looking down in the distance on the slag heaps of the mine which we had blown up two nights ago. It shimmered in the morning haze, and I could just imagine what scenes of activity and repair were going on inside. Presently we followed the path down to the main road at La Petite Verrière, the same road which had been picketed higher up. I left B and tip-toed cautiously till I could just glimpse the corner of the road through the trees. Everything was silent in the heat, but I was afraid there might be a German sentry standing in the shadow unseen. I watched for some time but could see nothing unusual. In the garden of the house opposite a woman was working unconcernedly — it seemed curious that anyone could be oblivious of the drama that was being played out in those silent woods. I ran back to collect B and we both sauntered across the road.

On the right was a large house and a farmyard this side of it, where there was another woman sweeping. We were still thirsty and anxious for information, so I went up to her and asked for a drink of water, and we got into conversation. When I asked her if she owned the big house next door, she looked at me in astonishment and said it was the Mairie. As this was the local police station we stayed on longer. Fate seemed determined to leave no stone of irony unturned.

We walked across the fields and came to a stream. Here I decided to make a proper effort to break our scent, so taking off our shoes we waded in the cool water. The stones were very hard on our feet as we walked upstream several hundred yards. Two lorries passed along the road in the meantime, but we were in the shade and could not be seen. We climbed out on the far bank, put on our shoes again and continued up through the trees. Presently we came to some more cultivated fields with a boy working in them. I stopped and chatted to him and asked if he would let us have some of the raw potatoes he was digging up, to eat; but he said he would have to ask his father first and he would not be back for an hour. He directed us towards Rousillon.

The next two hours were very exhausting, breaking our way through overgrown paths and dragging ourselves up steep hills. Brambles tore at our clothes and the sun was at the noon; the only consolation was the thought of making our pursuers sweat too. At last we struggled to the top and came out near some cottages. On the left was a rifle range and we could hear the German troops firing on it. We were pretty hungry, so I tried again to get some food. In the first house I entered was an old woman, very poor but quite sympathetic. I told her we were English, but she said she literally had nothing whatsoever to give us and after a glance round her kitchen I believed her. It seemed incredible but it was true — for we would have eaten anything, the rind out of the dust-bin or crumbs of bread on the floor, but there was nothing. She advised me to try next door where they had plenty.

I went in there and found the family at lunch round the table. They had the wireless on and were listening to the German controlled news. I could not have spoken openly before all of them and the young man had blond crinkly hair and gave me a hostile impression, so I made some routine inquiry and left again without asking for food. In time one comes to develop a certain intuition, a kind of sensitive antenna, in such matters; if a house had any unfriendly atmosphere whatsoever, I took no chances, for one only made one mistake.

We followed the road right through the centre of the village. I called out something about the heat to an old man standing in his doorway. We also spat frequently on the road. And so we continued all afternoon till five o'clock, occasionally passing people on the wayside, whom I usually greeted or stopped to pass the time of day with. We were taking a short cut across the fields when we came upon a group of woodcutters, two men and a boy. Again we stopped and chatted, but saw they were getting curious at my accent. I tried to take the man on one side and ask him for help, but every time I hinted I had something to say to him in private, he pretended not to understand my meaning. He was frightened of the boy and what he might repeat later. So I gave up the diplomatic struggle and we walked on. A little later, coming to a quiet stream, we stripped, washed and shaved, for I hoped to catch a train tomorrow. Once or twice we thought we heard the faint barking of dogs behind us in the woods — but I hoped it was our imagination.

We came out on the Route Nationale and followed it through Les Pasquelins. I had passed those same houses three months ago with H, and I should have called anyone mad who had foretold then that I should ever pass that way again. We left the road at the first opportunity and followed again little paths. We stopped often for rests, for we were tired. It was getting late and I knew we must get help soon. I had to find a pair of boots from somewhere, and we had to discover if there was still a bus running from Château Chinon. If there was not, we were utterly lost, for probably to-morrow they would have cast the net again all round this district. Soon we came to a little hamlet and I tried my luck at several cottages. Either there were too many people present or the atmosphere was not favourable enough to ask for help. I did find an old man grooming his horse in the yard. He was by himself except for a young child. I went up to him and spoke in general terms, then seizing my opportunity I whispered in his ear that we were English and would he help us. It was rather an anxious moment at that juncture to see which way the cat would jump. He peered into my face and clearly did not believe me. (All patriots in France have good reason to be suspicious of men claiming to be R.A.F. or English, as the Gestapo go to all lengths to find them out — even dropping English-speaking Germans by plane at night to trick the peasants into helping them.) Then he went off in a long tirade, how his son was a prisoner in Germany and times were hard, etc. etc. When I begged him again to help us, he turned away abruptly and went on with his work. There were people all around us in the cottages and I was only endangering him by staying. B had been stroking the horse all this time, serenely oblivious of the fatal ebb and flow of our conversation.

We left the yard and walked on. We had been rebuffed now so often that I was beginning to despair. Yet we had to get help that night. We were going along a small lane, when I saw five houses in a row. Outside the end one was a man working in the garden and I liked the honest look of his face. I left B in the hedge and went across to him. I spoke a little and then asked him for food. He shrugged his shoulders and said he had none and where was I from anyway. Then I looked him full in the face and said we were Englishmen. He asked me why I had picked on him to approach and I replied that we were desperate men and beggars could not be choosers. We continued to fence like this for about a quarter of an hour. Again B rested in the hedge, sublimely ignorant; the sun was beginning to go down behind the houses and the countryside lay hushed in the peace of evening. We might have been on a walking tour before the war; it seemed impossible to realize how our lives were at stake on the quiet conversation.

At last I managed to persuade him of our sincerity and he told me to follow him into his house. Here he explained how cautious he had to be, as he could trust none of his neighbours. The Gestapo had arrived in the middle of the night a week ago and searched his house for the crew of an R.A.F. bomber which had been shot down. A little before that three French prisoners of war who had escaped — French soldiers— had come after dark and asked by chance in the middle house for food. But the man there was a collaborationist, and while he kept them talking in the kitchen he sent his son out by the back door to betray them to the police. That was why he had wanted to know why I had chosen his house to approach. Truly a divine providence seemed to be guiding our steps.

I sat in his kitchen while his wife got together some food. He was about forty-five and had fought in the wars, and was a real patriot and could not do enough for us. He searched everywhere to find a pair of boots for me, but they were all too small. And I knew well what a sacrifice that meant in Europe today. He wrote out the times of buses and the hours of curfew in different departments. He offered to take us in himself to Château Chinon in the morning and put us on the bus. He dared not let us sleep in his house that night for fear of the neighbours talking. I think I shall always remember that Samaritan and his selfless charity. He brought some blacking and darkened my gym shoes to look like boots. When all was ready I went out; his wife shook hands and wished me all luck and we seemed like ships that pass in the night and seem to linger for an instant. I went and waited with B in the hedge, till the man brought us out a basket of food — two bits of salted bacon, some bread, and the last of his wine. When I passed him the empty basket back through the hedge I put a thousand franc note in it, but he indignantly handed it back. And then, without a word being spoken between us, he turned and went back into his cottage.

We waited a little in case someone should have seen us and then walked on. I had to stop a peasant and check my watch for the bus to-morrow, as of course we had no other way of verifying the time. On the brow of the hill two miles in front the houses and spires of Château Chinon stood out against the sunset like some heavenly city, the goal of these weary travellers. We walked on till it grew dark, then, turning into a cornfield, we settled down for the night. We ate the food and then, rolling up together in the one mackintosh on the dewy earth, we slept blissfully like children. It was cold outside, away from the heat of our bodies. We arranged that if the bloodhounds came up on us again during the night we would continue walking around Château Chinon till daylight and then nip in and catch the bus. Our last friend had warned me of the gendarmerie in the town, and I knew we would need all our wits and luck to escape.

Considering everything the night passed quite comfortably. We had taken off our suits and were lying on them to crease then smartly. Once or twice the cold woke me up and I looked out at the stars above us; once or twice a farm dog barked at the moon. The life of gipsies certainly has its attractions. At five a.m. we got up, as the bus left at seven-thirty and we had much to do. We dressed carefully in the dark and polished our shoes and brushed our clothes. We threw our revolvers away in the hedge. When all was completed we moved out on to the lane. I do not think that anyone would have taken us for men who had spent the last nine days in the woods. Lights were showing in the houses as we followed the track down to the river, but here it led us into a laundry and we could not get over. So we had to go back and make a long detour to the Route Nationale again. There we polished our shoes for the last time and then walked boldly down the road into the town. We passed a couple of men but they said nothing. When we got into the centre I asked the way to the bus stop, which was immediately opposite the gendarmerie. I bought the tickets for us both and we buried ourselves in the crowd waiting for the bus. Most of them smelt very strong themselves, so we passed unnoticed. It was light now and the German soldiers were getting up in the barracks opposite and standing about in the street, yawning and buttoning up their tunics. I hoped fervently there would be no police to check the papers.

After about thirty minutes of this suspense the bus arrived and we pushed our way in. I went right to the back and shoved B against the window so that nobody could talk to him. Just before we moved off two gendarmes climbed in with a Frenchman in handcuffs. This was rather a sobering sight. The prisoner was in his shirt-sleeves, as a man should be going to his execution. The journey to Nevers was uneventful and we arrived there about midday. Once or twice at the stops I saw figures in uniform at the side of the road and once they even came and looked in through the window. To sit down and rest on the seats had been bliss.

We got out opposite the railway station and I went in and bought our tickets, and then we sat in the park. The town was a divisional H.Q. and was full of German soldiers and airmen, young and arrogant looking. It seemed curious to be walking like this among one's enemies, against whom one would soon openly fight to the death on the great battlefields of the invasion. It was the *entr'acte* in a play or the procession before a bull fight, when the matador and bulls march together round the ring.

Later on we entered a bar, which I chose carefully as being the most empty. I sent B over to sit at a table in the corner and I went up and asked the woman behind the counter what we could have to drink. She looked at me for a moment and said that for us there was beer, though it was out of hours. After that rather startling introduction I took the glasses and resumed my seat. There was another man sitting opposite who, I noticed, was reading a German newspaper, so I did not like to continue the conversation further, but waited until he had gone. Then I had a long talk with the woman, who of course saw we were English. She spoke in contempt of the German soldiers passing outside on the pavement and warned us about all the latest travelling restrictions. She sent her waiter across to the station to check the time of our train. She produced a bottle of cognac to drink to our victory. B, like the English soldier

he was, turned his nose up in disgust at the cognac and
asked me to get him some more beer instead. But I trod on
his toe and told him the cause of our international relation-
ships demanded his self-sacrifice; speaking our own
language has its advantages at times. Some more people had
entered the bar meanwhile, so when we had emptied our
glasses we went out. As we passed the counter the woman
did not look up from her knitting.

The Paris train was full before it ever pulled into the
platform and we had to hammer the door of the corridor
down before we could break in. Then the besieging flood of
passengers surged into the crowded train by sheer force of
numbers amidst the cries and resistance of those already
standing in the corridor. The lavatory was piled high with
luggage and also had four people crammed inside. There
were children crying on the floor and there was no room
even to shift one's weight from one foot to the other.
Through the window streamed in the afternoon sun. We
stood thus for four hours to Paris and at the end of it I was
near fainting. The conditions of travelling have to be seen
to be believed — trains pull out of the stations leaving
crowds of frustrated people still on the platform, while
inside the half-empty compartments lounge at their ease
the masters of the German army. I am sure that it is these
petty injustices that inflame the hatred of a conquered people more than the far greater but remoter crimes.

We got out at the Gare du Nord, and mingled with the
crowd as it passed through the barriers, It did not pay to loi-
ter on railway stations, as they were always closely watched.
Outside there was a row of taxis, but as I was not positive
some of them were not private cars and, as I did not want to
risk an unnecessary conversation with my accent, we made
for the Metro. I went up in the queue to the window to buy
a book of tickets. I thought they cost eight francs and had a
ten franc note in my hand, but, when the man asked me for
thirteen francs, I had to grope wildly in my pocket book,
spilling out notes all over the counter and finally finding

nothing smaller than a thousand franc note. I felt everybody's eyes on me and the man behind the counter shot a
penetrating glance into my face. I seized the tickets and
almost ran down the stairs, but it was the same in the
Metro. We could hardly have looked more English; the
blacking had worn off my Army gym shoes, and I saw several people staring at them. The only thing was to stare back,
until they shifted uncomfortably too; nearly everybody in
France today has some skeleton in the cupboard.

We got out at the Rue Montmartre and went round to our
first safe house — a business address— only to find it had
just closed. This was a blow, and it now entailed our taking a
train out of Paris, and time was getting on. It was after seven
and curfew was at midnight. Anybody found out on the
streets after that would be arrested, and the whole trail of
our transgressions would be certain to come out. We took
the Metro again to the Gare St. Lazare, and changed on to
the suburban railway. After half an hour's journey we got out
at Sèvres, and I asked an old woman for our street. As it
turned out, she directed me to the wrong one, there being
two of the same name. So when we arrived at the right number and I gave the password to the woman who answered the
bell, she looked at me blankly — it clearly meant nothing to
her. One could never make too many inquiries, as this only
aroused curiosity and jeopardized the safety of the owners of
these houses, who had to live in that neighbourhood perma-
nently. So I apologised and we turned away.

Now we were in a desperate situation — lost in Paris,
with nowhere to go for the night, and only two hours left
before curfew. We had had nothing to eat all day and were
very thirsty. The time was nearly ten o'clock and the streets
were already deserted. After all our tribulations this was the
end. I tried one or two small hotels in the street for rooms,
but no one would take us in. There were two gendarmes in
one place drinking at the bar, so I did not enter. I asked a
woman in the street for help, and she advised me to ask in
the police station. I saw a church opposite, so we knocked

at the door of the priest's house, and I told the housekeeper we were two Belgian Catholics (to explain my accent) and had just arrived in Paris to find our friends gone. Could she shelter us for the night, otherwise the curfew...? She said the curé was away, and she could not take the responsibility; we had better try the hotels back in the city. In our desperation I promised silently that, should we ever escape, I would never refuse shelter to a beggar for the rest of my life.

We walked quickly to the Metro at the Pont de Sèvres a mile away. B's foot was hurting and we were both parched with thirst. By hurrying we just caught the last train of the night back to Paris. I remembered a hotel where I had stayed a night on my last journey three months ago. We had been strictly warned in London not to go near it, as it had been known by Mme C, who had subsequently been arrested by the Gestapo, but this was our last hope and I decided to risk it.

We came out of the Metro at Levallois after fort-five minutes. The streets were now pitch dark and empty. It was half an hour before curfew and, except for an occasional gendarme standing at the street corners, we were the only persons out at that late hour. I did not know the number of the house, but relied on recognizing it from the outside. I remembered that it stood on the corner. We hurried along the street, till we came to an open window. Inside the lighted room I could see eight people having supper round a table, and I was sure I recognized the face of one of the women as belonging to the family who ran the hotel I was looking for. So I banged on the street door till someone opened it. I suppose they thought we were the police or desperadoes, for the man's attitude could not have been more hostile. He asked me what I wanted, and I said a room for the night. He said he had none, and tried to shut the door. I was desperate, as I knew this was really our last hope, so I stuck my foot in the sill. I was still standing outside in the dark of the street, and I thought that perhaps he had not recognized me, so I tried to push my way in. There were other people crowding behind him in the lighted interior of the passage, so I could not be explicit. I said surely he remembered me staying there three months ago, but he only threatened to call the police, unless I left immediately, and began to shout; so I withdrew my foot and the door slammed in my face. As it turned out, my imagination must have played a strange trick on me, for I had mistaken the wrong hotel in the dark. Yet there was a mystery somewhere, because I swear I recognized that woman's face through the lighted window.

We continued along the street to the next corner, where stood another hotel, the right one, but probably the Germans had seized it since my last visit. I left B in the street and rang the bell in some suspense. While I listened to the footsteps on the other side, I prayed wildly to the Little Flower to save us, for I was tired and hungry and frightened again, and had no desire any longer to be a martyr.

The door opened and we passed into the dimly lit courtyard. It was an old coaching inn and the proprietor was a typical Frenchman, rather fat, with a round face and a thick moustache, and a blue apron tied round his waste. He could barely see our faces in the dark, but I whispered in his ear asking him for help, reminding him I had stayed there three months ago, and that we were English. To my unspeakable joy he recognized my voice and we were home.

He was another of the real patriots of France. He gave us a room each, and went off and cooked us some food himself. He returned with bread, and eggs, and some red wine. He was delighted to see me again, and clapped me enthusiastically on the back. To be at last among real friends, and to have a bed and a roof over one's head, was an unforgettable experience. We were soon fast asleep between the sheets.

PARIS (AUGUST 25TH TO 29TH)

Next morning our host brought us each up to our rooms a steaming bowl of coffee. I lay in the warm bed, and thought that life could never bring me any greater happiness. The coloured curtains of my room fluttered in the morning sunshine, and through the open window came the voices of people passing in the street underneath and the clatter of the carts over the cobbled stones. This was the Paris I loved, and the memory of that morning was an ample reward for all our dangers and hardships. Man lives on contrast — we had passed through the valley of death, and life was now all the more desirable, because we had once despaired of it.

I took B to lunch round the corner at a 'black market' restaurant, where of course we sat in silence all through the meal. In the afternoon he went back to bed, and I took his shoes and went off to contact the headquarters of the organization. I was admitted into a tailor's shop and found the man whom I was seeking. I then went round and saw D, who was being sheltered in a hotel. He was hunched up in bed in a tiny room, and looked overwrought. He had not slept a night, since he had left me that afternoon at the farm two hundred miles away, and was delighted to hear of the success of our mission. He had now only one thing more to look forward to — our return as soon as possible to England, and his newly married wife and the child to be born. I shook hands and went out of the room, and never saw him since, nor will I. A week later the Gestapo broke into the hotel before dawn, while they were all in bed, and arrested him and his host.

Two hours later B and I completed the last stage of our travelling in Paris, when we were taken to another and safer house in the suburbs. We arrived at nightfall and received a royal welcome. Our hosts opened a bottle of champagne from the stock they were keeping against the Day, and we all drank to the speedy coming of the Allies. In the wonder and joy of the faces round the table, I could see how unbelievable it was to them to see English soldiers again in France, and I knew what great tidings it was our privilege to bring. One night a lady came in and sat at the table talking with us till late into the night. The next day she said to our host: 'I know it sounds fantastic and ridiculous, but I suddenly got the feeling that those two men in your house last night were Englishmen. But then I thought again and realized, of course, it could not be so.'

Another afternoon we were in Janine's drawing room, while she was playing Beethoven's Appassionata on the piano, when the front door bell went. We watched her go to the gate and next minute, to our horror, saw the helmet of a policeman enter. We fled to the bottom of the garden, and only heard later the sequel to the story. He was apparently a friend of Janine's and a staunch sympathizer of de Gaulle's, like many of the police. She told him he could not come into the house, as she had some friends in; he said he thought he knew them; but she was sure he did not. Then he told her in confidence that the war was going very well, and he had been told that there were many English parachutists in the country. What he would have said, if he had known there were two then inside the house, I cannot imagine.

There was a constant stream of visitors all day, and we were for ever bolting upstairs, or peering through the curtain at the company in the garden. Men in uniform came sometimes, and there was one man who was certain that Germany would win the war. One day a barber came to cut B's hair and, as B could not speak one word of French, our host explained to the haircutter that B was a sailor and dumb. At the end, the man said, what a shame it was for a young man like that to have lost the power of speech.

In the evenings I would sit on the sofa and listen, while Janine caressed from the piano the melodies of Chopin, and the wilder and grander music of Beethoven, and sang charming folk songs of Old France. And we talked in between of Anatole France, and idealism, and monks, and poverty. Janine was only twenty-one, but had already played on the radio, and given her own concerts in the biggest halls of Paris. It seemed such a fantastic contrast to the sound. I was sure that the others must have fallen in the village and either been caught or given the alarm (as indeed they nearly did.) I entered a small wood and there stripping I dug a hole by the light of a shaded torch and buried my parachute and equipment. Then putting on my macintosh and hat I returned to the road. At 4 o'clock I left the hill and went to the rendezvous, where the road ended at the edge of the village and a path went up between the woods. I lay down by the edge of a stream and drank greedily. The singing of the birds was continuous and I thought how much Julian Stonor would have loved to be here. One experienced somehow — however incongruously — a great sense of freedom. 3

Paris May 1943

September 1943

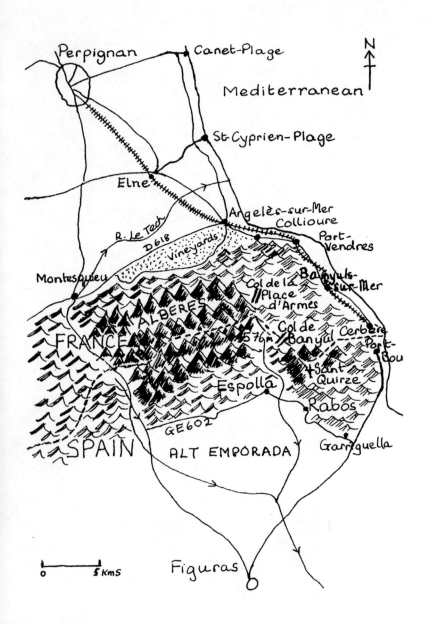

men who, only a few days before, had been fleeing for their
lives and been tracked by bloodhounds through the forests.

THE ESCAPE TO SPAIN AND HOME

September 1943

On Sunday night B and I caught the train down from Paris
to the south. It was packed out, and for a long time we had
to stand in the crowded corridor. After a while somebody
poked his head out of a carriage, and offered us a seat which
had not been claimed. As the man was very talkative, I
took the seat myself, for I did not like to risk B inside even
to share it later on. I sat squashed up between the man and
a girl in the corner, and read Janine's copy of Baudelaire so
as to avoid being dragged into the conversation. About
eleven p.m. at long last someone turned the carriage lights
out, and we settled down for the night. I was wearing the
borrowed shoes, which were far too small, and I was in considerable pain. My feet burned all the time, and I wondered
how I was going to last out the night. I kept my eyes always
on the corridor to make certain that B was all right, and no
one was speaking to him. If that happened, I had arranged
to get up myself, and to say that he had had a bad accident
and a paralytic shock, and was struck dumb. As that might
have to be our story, I naturally told him in no circumstances must he be seen talking to me all the time we were
in the train together. Everything had to be done by signs.

Suddenly, while the train was still running, a German
Gestapo official in uniform entered the carriage, turned on
the lights and demanded to see all our papers. He wore
glasses, and had a square torch clipped to his tunic, and
imparted a great atmosphere of fear and malevolence. I
showed him my card and, after one look at me, he handed it
back. But to my horror, when he reached B in the corridor,
he examined the back of his card closely for several seconds
(it was of course forged), and then I heard him ask B something in French. As he could not speak a single word, my

heart nearly stopped beating, and I was on the point of getting up out of my seat and intervening, as I had promised. Meanwhile B, like the farmer's son he was, just shrugged his shoulders and continued to stare at the floor. The German gave him a contemptuous glance, as though he could not waste time talking to such an illiterate oaf when he had still the whole train to examine, and passed on down the corridor. It was one of the worst moments of my travels.

The rest of the night passed uneventfully, and the girl slept most of the time with her head on my shoulder. The train kept on stopping at different stations, and more gesticulating and shouting people poured in each time. B was almost suffocated in the passage, and had to stand all night.

At ten a.m. we got out at Narbonne, and spent the day in the park and the cinema, while all the arrangements with the guides were made. At evening we took the train on again to Perpignan, where we had some food in the railway buffet. It was a typical summer's evening, very hot and dusty and still. There were three German soldiers eating at the next table, and, with freedom so near, I could not help looking at them very contemptuously. Towards dark we set out walking through the streets, following the guide who was wheeling a bicycle, past the German barracks, and out into the country. Here we turned off the main road into the vineyard, where our guide who would be taking us over the mountains into Spain was waiting. We took the sacks of food and put on our rope sandals, and a few minutes later set out into the night.

After walking for ten minutes our guide told us to wait for him, while he disappeared again ahead. I lay on my back in the cool night air, knowing from before the wisdom of seizing any such rest, while B groped among the vines looking for bunches of grapes. Presently the guide returned with two other men, and two women, and some more food to carry. This made our party up to nine, and was an unheard-of size for this dangerous crossing of the Pyrenees near the sea. I, as an experienced traveller, was very dubious of the whole proceedings, but this was clearly not the time to start an argument. That could wait till morning.

We put the women in front, and we set off at a fast walking pace. We men took turns at carrying the food, and later the baggage of the women too, who had brought an absurd amount for so difficult a route. It was hard enough to heave oneself over those hills, as I knew, without any additional burdens. I brought up the rear, carrying the loaves of bread balanced on my shoulder. This pace we kept up without a pause all night.

For the next three hours our route led on through the vineyards and the fields, past farms and lighted windows, along main roads, always moving parallel to the mountains towards the sea. The women were already at this early hour exhausted by the remorseless pace, and kept on falling behind at every obstacle — at each stream or ditch. Then they would get nervous of losing contact with the guide, as he disappeared in the distance in front, and kept on crying out in the silence of the night. And we would have to seize them by the arm and hurry them along the tracks, stumbling and falling every so often, until they were almost in despair, and their skirts and stockings were torn to shreds. It can be imagined what a noise this procession made and, when we came to the river, the rattle of the slipping stones set all the dogs barking on the farms, and they continued to bark for an hour. Our experiences with the bloodhounds had rather upset my nerves, and I kept on listening for the sounds of any pursuit.

At midnight we stopped for a quarter of an hour and smoked cigarettes in the undergrowth, shielding the glow from the direction of the mountains. The women threw themselves down and went fast asleep, and the little clearing was soon full of our snores. In a few minutes we were up and on again. I changed the bread for a sack of food, which I slung over my shoulder; its whiteness served as a useful guide to the man behind. We were all getting fairly thirsty. Our guide warned us we were now entering the prohibited zone, and we must move with extreme silence, as there might be German patrols about.

Presently we came to the line of the railway, and had to scramble down the cutting and across the live rails. The lights of the station were only a few hundred yards away to the right and on the left was a signal box. We made a terrible clatter getting across, but fortunately everybody must have been asleep. A bit farther on we passed the last vineyards before entering the mountains and, pausing an instant, we groped greedily in the dark for bunches of grapes to slake our thirst. They were wonderfully cool and sweet to the lips, and the profusion of that vineyard in the moonlight beneath the dark mass of the Pyrenees was an unforgettable memory. We cut some more bunches and wrapped them in a handkerchief.

On we went again, and continued without a pause all through the rest of the night. The guide was racing the dawn, as he knew he had to be at a certain covered valley by daylight. The pace was cruel and the burdens heavy, and the women of course in despair, crying that they would never have come, had they known it was such an ordeal. It was dark under the mountains, and we kept on stumbling and falling on the goat-tracks. Ever we climbed as the hours passed — until we finally stopped in a cleft with high ground all around. It was light now, and there were dogs barking above us. I thought the guide had misjudged his timing, and we had arrived here too late and alarmed the German patrols. While the barking of the dogs came nearer, the others lay motionless on the rocks and held their breath. B was so exhausted he fell asleep immediately and began to snore until someone kicked him...Through the undergrowth above I could see the legs of a man walking, and heard him calling to the dogs. The guide asked me was it the Gestapo or the farmer, but I could not see to say. The next ten minutes were full of suspense, and I remembered thinking how ironic it was to have come so far, and to have escaped so many perils already, and to be caught now at the eleventh hour on the threshold of freedom. I cursed the guide again for his temerity in continuing the march so late.

Then we heard footsteps coming down the path towards us. Then I saw a man stop and turn on an irrigation tap, and the next minute a torrent of water flooded down the rocks on top of us. We had to move quickly out of the way, and of course the man saw us and called out. I thought it was the end, for even if he were not a German, the farmers in those parts would be far too frightened of the mountain guards to help and hide us from them. They would be sure to hand us over, if only to save their own lives. The guide left us and went down to talk to the man in Catalan, and we could only sit at a distance and watch their gesticulations. We were all far too exhausted to run, and escape was impossible anyway in the daylight.

Fortunately in the end the guide succeeded in pacifying the farmer, and we saw them even smoking together. Perhaps it was all a put up job from the beginning to get more money out of us — you can never tell in the Pyrenees. Later on he and his wife came up with a basket of figs and almonds and a pot of coffee, which was very welcome.

We spent the whole day lying under the bushes in the valley and sleeping, as the guide warned us we had a stiff night's climb ahead. There was a fresh spring of water at hand, and the day was hot, and the bed of earth was very enjoyable to our tired bodies. One looked back, down over the foothills we had climbed to France. On the right sparkled the Mediterranean.

The feet of the women were in a very bad way with blisters. We dressed them as best we could and made them as comfortable as possible, and gave them some of our food, bread and hunks of meat. The figs were very refreshing. We had to lie absolutely quiet and ensure that our coats and shirts did not show through the bushes, as the Germans patrolled round the head of the valley above us every afternoon. I lay and read Baudelaire, while T went and talked to the women and the two men, and learnt their story. Both were married couples who had been working for de Gaulle in the underground movement, inside France for the last year. One of the men had been in charge of the Intelligence Service, and the other was his wireless operator. The fair-haired woman with a very dominant, and rather unpleasant, personality had been a courier. All of them had lived very dangerously for the last nine months; the operator used to transmit messages while the other patrolled round the house with a tommy gun. Eventually the Germans had got on their trail, and they had only just got away in time. They were now on their way back to England, the land of promise flowing with milk and honey, for good, and were busy planning their future. They had taken on the job from the men before, and other people would be continuing it now — only the individuals changed; nine months was a long time to have lasted in the field.

Towards evening there was thunder and the sky darkened. I knew from before what storms meant in those mountains, and was fearful of the coming night. It seemed inhuman to take the women on again.

We set off at dusk. I was carrying the sack over my shoulders. The guide made the women put a pullover over their blouses, as he did not want the white to show in the dark, for we would be crossing between the frontier posts tonight. After we had been climbing up the rocks about half an hour, during which time the women had to be literally pulled up each yard of the ascent, I halted the party, for below us in the valley I could see some men moving. We stopped a few minutes and watched them walking under trees like insects. They were probably shepherds tending the mountain goats, but it was impossible to tell at that distance. Anyway I think we were all glad of the rest.

Soon the mist began to swirl round us in the hills, and it was safe to go on. I hoped the guide would not lose the way. After ascending a little further almost sheer up the rock face, the blonde-haired woman complained of giddiness, and had to lie down on the ledge for a while. I began to think it was madness bringing them over the mountains, and I did not see how we were ever going to get across. The guide would not wait long, but hurried on to get the light of the moon before it set. No one without experience of the Pyrenees can appreciate what difference the moon makes at night.

On and up we went towards the summit over the rocks and boulders. I had the sack of bread on my back, and was leading the quieter of the two women by one hand and tapping my way with a stick in the other. We were going along a knife-edge, and on the left was a sheer drop over the rocks below. Every now and again we had to skirt the German observation posts a few hundred feet above us on the peaks, and then again there was no path at all, but just a precipitous scramble over the boulders in the dark. As we approached the final summit of the Pyrenees, there was a great wind roaring in our faces. It was very dark now, and every few minutes there was thunder and forked lightning across the sky. We were right in the middle of a magnetic storm, and the whole picture was very impressive. One minute one would be stumbling in the dark, and next the whole peak around would be lit like daylight in the flash of lightning. Below us down by the sea there was a great fire burning, whose glow reddened the whole sky like a false dawn, and what caused it we were never able to discover. The women were naturally very frightened and kept on crying and falling in the dark. Their legs were bruised and cut on the rocks, and everything was in tatters. It was indeed a very eerie scene; the noise of the wind, which buffeted one's face, drowned every other sound, and drove one back into one's own thoughts. One moved on steadfastly like an automaton, and ceased to have any affinity or connection with one's fellow travellers. Each of us was shut off and had his own battle to fight against the elements, except when every few minutes the varying pressure of the woman's hand in mine, as we both swayed and stumbled in the gale, recalled me to the scene.

And so we went on again all the night through, up and

down the ridges, and then descending again into the dark of the valleys. The moon threw a grey light, which gave everything a colourless and unearthly appearance. After about four hours, in the middle of the night, the men could go no farther and, falling down, refused absolutely to go on. They were at the limits of physical exhaustion. After a year in Occupied Europe they naturally had not the stamina; they were weak and tired to death, and said they would rather be taken by the Germans than go on. So the guide had to agree, and we all threw ourselves down on the rocks and fell into instant sleep. I lay on my back, and stared at the rocks around. The effects of the moonlight on the stony scene had all the apocalyptic unearthliness of an El Greco painting. Near to the limits of human endurance, I thought of the words of that Indian mystic: 'If there is a Hell on earth, it is here, it is here, it is here.'

B complained that his ankle was burning, but I told him sharply to shut up. Up here, on the frontier of the Pyrenees, with the Germans all around us, this was not the time for complaints. Men before now had been brought over those mountains with broken legs — and even if he were dying he must go on. The guide told me that it was near here some weeks ago that, as he was leading another party over the frontier, a man had suddenly stepped out from behind a rock in the night and challenged them, and how he and one other had run and escaped, and how the Germans had fired at them and set their dogs after them. This was clearly no place to linger.

In a few minutes he ordered us on again and urged the utmost silence for the next hour, unless we all wanted to be caught. The moon had set, but we could get some idea of how the ground lay by the reflection of the fire. Up we went over the crest into the teeth of the icy wind, each man locked tight in the ivory tower of his own mind.

We scrambled down a wooded dell and crossed a stream at the bottom, leaving a German post a few hundred yards on our right. Suddenly we heard a crashing behind us in the bushes, and everybody scattered. But it turned out to be, not a patrol, but only one of the women who had fallen behind and got lost. The guide went back for her. Then we came out into the open again, and saw before us the last ridge, on whose summit lay the frontier of Spain. As I climbed up the last stretch of our journey into freedom, arm in arm with one of the women who was near fainting with exhaustion, and as the wind blew cold and fresh on our faces, I told her to feel on her cheeks *'le vent de la liberté'*. From the top we looked down the farther side at lights of Spain. Here once again I stood outside the gates of German Europe, though this time I had left comrades behind me in the prison.

We walked down a little to a brook, where we drank greedily and rested. Cigarettes were lit and silence was at an end. We talked excitedly and no longer in whispers, for we were free men again. Later on, as it began to grow light, we walked on another mile or so to our final resting place for the day on the side of the hill under the cover of some trees. This was a sort of regular half-way house for the guides, and in the ashes of previous fires there were relics of the travellers who had passed that way before.

The day passed rather like an idyll, sleeping round a log fire which we lit. There was not much to eat, but it was very peaceful after the night before. Later on we all went down to a spring in the cool of the evening and washed our feet. Far below us in the distance one could just see the houses of Figueras, our goal for the night, the longest march of all; but I was very dubious whether the women could make it, as they could hardly hobble. While we were sitting about waiting for it to grow dark, the guide was telling me how some time ago he went at night to the usual rendezvous in the vineyard back in France, and there was given four men to take over the mountain, and all the customary arrangements were made. After they had been walking for an hour with the guide leading, he suddenly felt a pistol stuck in his back, and turning round realized he had been betrayed and the four men were from the Gestapo. He was taken back to Perpignan and thrown into prison, where he would have been executed in time, had he not escaped a week before. He was now back again at his dangerous trade.

Francesco, as he was called, like all the mountain guides, had fought in the civil war for the Reds, and was a wanted man on both sides of the frontier, and the money which he earned — a considerable amount by European standards— seemed comparatively useless, as he could never risk going into the towns to spend it. He had a young wife, who was very attractive, and did not seem to belong to the hard life of the hills.

As the sun was setting we started out. The loads were lighter to carry, and the end of the journey was actually in sight, though to-night was to be the longest ordeal of the three. A great silence had fallen in the mountains. We walked fast, and as long as we maintained that speed the women were forced to ignore their blistered feet to keep up. I had one of them by the arm and was hurrying her along the road, and so had little time to appreciate the changing shades of colour as night fell in these long-to-be-remembered hills.

We left the track at the bottom and plunged down the broken ground in the dark. At the end of one field we had to stop for ten minutes, while a man drove his cattle home for the night. Then down and up again over the many ridges. We were all very thirsty, and the effect of our fitful sleep during the day soon wore off, and weariness returned to our limbs. The night's march stretched ahead again with all its demands on the will and endurance.

At the top of the next hill the husbands of the two women, who were if anything more exhausted than their wives, and had no one to console them, cried out they could go no farther and flung themselves on the ground. So we all rested a little on the stones. We gave the women a drug to keep them going. After a few minutes we pulled each other up and continued, and so on again with the

same routine all night. The going is so difficult and varied
in the Pyrenees that one can never fall into the rhythm of
walking, but must concentrate all the time on the ground at
one's feet. One comes to long for the approach of daylight
as heralding the end of the march — but how slowly those
hours pass! I suppose we walked for ten hours each of the
three nights and must have covered in all the best part of
one hundred miles.

After midnight we came out on the level land once more
and entered the first vineyards in Spain. The grapes were
very sweet and we tore greedily at the clusters to slake our
thirst. They had all been sprayed with some preparation,
which it was impossible to see in the dark, but which gave
several of us acute diarrhoea later one. At a track junction
our guide left us, while he went on into the village to buy
some wine. We slept heavily in the moonlight, our snores
echoing over the quiet fields. The air was cold, and my feet
ached in their borrowed shoes. After two hours the guide
returned with some bottles of fire-water which was quite
undrinkable by anyone but himself. We continued the way
now along the roads in a thick mist. Presently we passed
through a village, where the street lights shone on the
brown earthen walls. It was about three o'clock in the
morning. Suddenly two men came bicycling out of the mist
towards us, and we all dived into a ditch on the side of the
road. The ditch was full of water, there was a terrible noise
of splashing, and the two men turned out in the end to be
Spanish workmen and not frontier guards. But still they
might have easily been our enemies, and I think Francesco
took unwarrantable risks. But such men are fatalists, I suppose, and are confident of their own powers of escape. We
climbed wearily up out of the ditch and went on again.
Leaving the village and the road we struck out across the
fields again. Presently we came to a river dark with tall
reeds and crumbling banks. It took us twenty minutes to
push and pull the party over, and I had to flounder across
carrying one of the women on my back. Crashing through

the reeds, and tearing my trousers when we fell, it was really more of a nightmare than a romance. We had to cross the same river again higher up, but this time it was over a swaying rope bridge. We came out on a main road, and I at the rear of the file just crossed it a few minutes before a farm cart creaked past. It was just beginning to get light, and we would have looked a curious procession to any farmer. We passed below the fort of Figueras and under the same viaduct where I had passed three months ago with G and the others. Bugles were sounding the hour of reveille, and outside there were men stirring in the fields.

The pace was now cruel and the mirage of a farmhouse — our journey's end— was always held out as just round the next corner or over the next rise. T was carrying all the men's packs himself, as no one else was capable of carrying anything. The guide was leading one woman by the arm, and I had the other. The women could not ever have walked upright unaided, and even with our help kept on falling down and going over on their ankles. Several times they had implored us to leave them where they fell to the mercies of the Spanish police. It was really terrible to witness their sufferings, which were hard enough even for fit men to endure. It was heart breaking to witness the crucifixion of those two women. It made one, Englishman that one was, realize the price of liberty and how little it is valued in our land. I wonder how many Englishwomen of their age would have faced the agony of those night marches in the hills.

At last we stumbled into the farmyard and up a ladder into the loft, where the eight of us threw ourselves down on the straw and rested our bleeding feet. Presently the farmer brought us up some water to wash in and a bowl of soup, and afterwards we slept. It made one realize how beyond all price are the common things of life.

Outside, the hot Spanish day wore on, until in the afternoon sleep became impossible. We just lay and sweated in the straw, and scratched at all the vermin in our hair. The communal lavatory was the wall of the open courtyard beneath. Flies buzzed everywhere in the loft, and the hens kept on clucking their way up the ladder and running in to lay eggs in the corner. The women were naturally disgusted at the squalor, even more so being French, and sent out to try and buy some underwear in the village. In the evening we went down in turn and had a meal in the kitchen, which was bare and dirty to a degree. There was hardly any light in there, and one could not even see what one was eating, and the heat was suffocating. The farmer and his wife did their best for us but, like all Spanish peasants, they were terribly poor, and they had never known anything better than this squalor.

Afterwards we went and sat outside against the wall and talked to the farmer in the moonlight, while the cool breeze ebbed through the vineyards. Behind us in the mountains flashed the lightning of the magnetic storm which had continued for four nights.

Two days passed thus in the barn waiting for the next arrangements to be made. The time passed pretty interminably playing cards and sleeping. We had to keep back from the window so as not to be seen by any passers-by, and we could only talk in whispers. Our guide and his wife used to come up periodically and bring in bananas and grapes, which were very welcome in that heat. We all told tales of our experiences in France, and I think that the two married men were very grateful to us for bringing their wives over the mountains. The guide swore he would never take women again, but among those who fight the Germans there is a great equality and comradeship. We were privileged to have the opportunity of helping them and our cause.

The second day the two couples left, and we followed the day after. A taxi arrived for us at midday, and we hurried across the ploughed fields to the road. The countryside was sleeping in the noontide heat and we saw no one. Doubling and sweating after our twenty minutes' run, we just arrived at the rendezvous in time. The taxi was waiting with engine running and the door open, and we jumped in as it moved off. Two cars had been caught recently by the Spanish police waiting for illegal passengers who had crossed the frontier, and the penalty was death.

We drove for two hours, passing several carabinieri on the side of the road, and finally stopped in a deserted stretch by some woods. Here we got out quickly and were led down a path, and eventually to a big house on the edge of the village. We entered in, and the civilization of its interior was like an Aladdin's cave after our last few days. There was unlimited food, wine, baths, and beds with sheets, and the latest papers. The house was owned by a Frenchwoman who was a great patriot. She had lived there all through the war, helping her countrymen in their escape over the mountains. Those who were caught and sent to Spanish prisons she used to visit daily, and bring them food, and interceded for them. We were among real friends at last. That night she gave us all a tremendous dinner, and we drank to the resurrection of France in Marsala wine.

The next day we travelled into Barcelona by train, where we spent the rest of the week hiding in a house, cramped up three in a tiny room. The shutters had been drawn all day so that we should not be seen, and the only interest was to watch through the chinks the men working on the opposite side of the street. How monotonous were those days and how interminable, from each morning to the night. And yet thousands of people in Occupied Europe live every day underground in similar captivity.

On the fifth night we drove down to Madrid, where we changed our prison for the Embassy. Here I learnt that the four men, who were to cross the mountains on the same route immediately after us, had all been caught by the Germans. They were being driven in a lorry outside Perpignan, when it had broken down with engine trouble, and a police patrol had come along the road and arrested the lot.

We used to pace up and down the courtyard of the Embassy like animals in a cage, which was our only chance of exercise — forty paces of it. I was growing tired of this captivity and longed for the sweetness of freedom. Also in the Embassy were some American and R.A.F. pilots, who had been shot down in France, and escaped. One, a Spitfire pilot, had wandered around France for a year trying to get out, and when he had called on his father in Paris for help, he found that he was collaborating with the Germans, and was ordered to leave the house immediately. Another had married a French girl after being shot down, and she had escaped with him into Spain. Another was an American, the pilot in a Flying Fortress which had been shot down in broad daylight over Paris. He had been hit by three cannon shells in the leg. When he bailed out, his parachute would not open, and as he fell he fed it out himself with one hand from its bag. He landed near a wood, and a few seconds later a Frenchman ran up, helped him out of his parachute, which they hid, took his uniform off and gave him a suit of old clothes, and concealed him in the bushes. Here he had to remain in the open for two days without food or water, as the Germans were searching for him with sheep dogs. Meanwhile, with his wounds undressed gangrene was setting in.

After two days the farmer came back, and eventually brought him to Paris, and handed him over to an organization. They hid him in an attic of a surgeon's house, where he was operated on and the bullets removed from his leg. Here he lay for four weeks with a German brewery just outside the window on the opposite side of the street. One day the maid, who all this time had no idea he was in the house and whose patriotism was suspect, caught sight of him by accident, and he had to be moved at once to another house across Paris. His leg was still unhealed and it had been agony walking on it in the Underground. Eventually after two months he travelled south, and in a party of fourteen set out over the Pyrenees. They were led across the mountains of Andorra, which is the safest but longest route. They had to climb up to the snow line over the highest passes nine thousand feet up. Once or twice men in the party lost their footing in the dark and fell over the rocks below and were never seen again. One man in the rear lost his way and disappeared and, though the guide went back and looked for him for two days, they never found him. Out of the original party of fourteen only eleven arrived in Spain. They took nine days on the journey, and suffered a lot from thirst on the way.

He said he would never face that crossing again. His own wounds had reopened after the second day and he could walk no farther; so the guides had left him up in a village for a week and collected him again, when they passed that way with the next party.

On the third day we travelled down to Gibraltar under assumed names.

I arrived at Gibraltar at four in the afternoon and left by plane for England that night. The aerodrome at Gibraltar was swept by searchlights of the Rock, which threw thin rays of light from the face of the dark towering mass above us and gave one the impression of some Wagnerian Rhine castle. I remembered that I had dined at the Governor's house in Berlin when he was military attaché there before the war.[1]

We took off at midnight and touched down in Scotland for breakfast. Once again I was home.

CHAPTER FOUR

PREPARING FOR INVASION

RETURN AND AWARD

September 1943

I arrived home in London from France, and I spent the next fortnight interviewing various people and writing

---

[1] Lieutenant General F N Mason MacFarlane, D.S.O.

my report. The R.A.F. were going to send Mosquito aircraft to complete our work by bombing the whole plant and photographing the previous damage. It was great fun to be rid of all those drab suits and to wear uniform again and to be a typical guardsman. I was told that I would not be allowed to go abroad again until the invasion — and then in uniform. I had lived under the death penalty for a year now with my nerves always tensed for impending operations and it was a great relief to have that sword lifted at last.

One night I saw A again in a dream (whom the bloodhounds had caught with the others after we parted that night in the woods). It was inside some sort of factory with great machines running. He and two others were standing on a trolley with rails round the edge of it. He was wearing a dark suit and his skin was like parchment. As he was wheeled past me I saw the expression of his face, which was impassive and vacant like some Egyptian mummy. His eyes rested on me for an instant, but they stared through me to the wall. I had the sensation he was blind. I woke up instantly, sweating with horror at that memory.

October 1943

I went back for six weeks to the 2nd battalion in Yorkshire. Here, through some misunderstanding which was in fact very near the truth, I had been given up as missing and Masses had been said for me at Ampleforth—so I was treated rather as a ghost at the beginning.

It was very consoling to hear the good wishes of the guardsmen again — to see the lights of a tented camp shining diaphanous in the dark, to sit in the warm secure atmosphere of a sing-song concert, to hear bugle calls and the music of men marching, to follow the red twinkling lights of an armoured column on a night march, to lie again in the dark of a bivouac beside a Sherman tank and to listen to the language of guardsmen, to sit at supper in the covered back of a three-ton truck in the harbour area and to talk to one's fellow officers of life in Paris six weeks ago, while from outside through the flaps came the immortal hissing of the petrol cookers — to the last night ride in the carriers with Guardsman Murphy beside me at the wheel, when I drove the forty-one miles back to camp under the freezing stars.

One morning Julian and I walked down the valley to Rievaulx, whose ruined arches framed the blue sky, sleeping eternally in that quiet place. On my last night we drove over together to Ampleforth and dined in the silence of the monks' refectory and listened to the plain chant of Vespers and later to the carefree laughter of boys. I realized then better than ever how much I was fighting for.

November 1943

I received today in the *London Gazette* the award of the D.S.O. which has in a kind of way set the official seal on the whole of my last year's work. I suppose now that this is the first step on the road to fame, little though I care for it. I feel genuinely reluctant that the old days of irresponsible privacy and the delights of remaining incognito have somehow gone for ever, for I know very well where this path is leading and that there can be no turning back. And when I think of D and the other four who died as the price of our success, I remember the bitterness of Alain Gerbault after the last war at the returning survivors 'ostentatiously displaying those medals commemorating the victories that really belonged to the dead'.

A report had been received from the field confirming our damage at the mine and stating that fires were raging there a week afterwards.

A MOST IMPORTANT CROSSROAD

December 1943

And now again, as these missions are entirely voluntary, I have been offered the opportunity of leaving this work and returning to my battalion, and for the third time I have made the decision to stay and this time to the end. Each time all my own inclinations have pulled me back to the

Irish Guards and still more so now that the hour of fighting at last approaches, and I know only too well how I shall yearn next April to be back in the comradeship of the battalion, where I have constantly returned as to my home.

But each time I come to make the decision I realize more clearly what the work it is I am doing and the importance of my mission. In the beginning it was chiefly a desire for activity in the war and the curious attraction of self-sacrifice. Ever since the night of the Channel action of the destroyers against a German merchant cruiser[t] when for the first moment of the war I knew what it was to live, I realized that I could never settle back to the routine of Salisbury Plain. I remembered always seeing that night from the bridge how dark the outline of the coast of France lay against the moonlight on the sea and I wondered what went on behind that impenetrable wall, as mysterious and remote as that of another planet. Occasionally messages had come from the other side; I had read the cry of an underground paper in Denmark: 'Come quickly or we perish, for the waters of Hell have risen to our lips.' And again somewhere at the back of my mind, like the romantic tale of Richard the First's captivity, was the idea that if he were alive anywhere in Europe I might one day meet Michael Marks[tt].

But as the time passed and I travelled abroad and saw what went on on the far side of that impenetrable wall, I came to appreciate what our real role was. One half of our mission was the economic importance of the target we aimed to destroy, and thus the shortening of the war and the saving of soldiers' lives later, in co-ordination with the strategic programme of industrial paralysation by the R.A.F. And it was a great triumph of scientific ingenuity when one realized how much a few trained men could effect with

[t] Through an inter-service liaison scheme, Hugh Dormer made a trip on a destroyer in October 1942. See Appendix for his account of this.
[tt] An Oxford friend, reported missing after a bombing raid, later known to have been killed.

explosives; for our charges were placed accurately on the vital part of our target, while the R.A.F. could only plaster the general area and might miss the nerve centre of an industrial plant completely.

The other half of our mission as I saw it was the encouragement to the French patriots that our deeds brought. To strike daringly and to defy the Germans openly inside their own fortress evoked for me memories of Drake and the Elizabethans. And I am sure that wherever we went afterwards and in whatever houses we were sheltered in our travels through France, we brought great faith and consolation. For, as I said before, the Channel lay between our two countries like the end of the world, and no man knew what was stirring across those waters. England through Continental eyes was now more than ever the *Ultima Thule* of Roman times. Ever since 1940 and the not too inspiring spectacle of Dunkirk no English soldiers had been seen on the Continent, and men's memories were growing a little dim and clouded with bitterness, for the Germans and the fear of the Gestapo lay everywhere like silence over the land, and resistance seemed hopeless and was paid for dearly in blood. And so we were welcomed as the forerunners of the Allied armies of liberation, just as the R.A.F. passing overhead through the night skies were honoured as the only ambassadors of England left abroad. When they were shot down and their graves were heaped with flowers, they too, did they but know it, played a role that was far more important than the material destruction of their raids.

And then in the wider sphere, too, our travels had a political significance. For I am certain that what goes on in the underground warfare of Europe now will play as large a part in determining the post-war role of those countries as the deeds of their soldiers and the fate of the battlefields to come. On the central stage of France many countries and many factions are staking their claims to the future and, when the great landings in the West take place, the measure of patriot support will determine whether France is to be great again or not — and all that follows from that answer. As Cardinal Verdier pointed out, it is the soldiers without uniform risking their lives now in sabotage and resistance who are the real heroes of France today.

All these ideas are only slowly receiving official recognition over here. When I first joined the organization a year ago, it had the sordid and unhealthy atmosphere of some secret society — there was little idealism or nobility about it; and for a long time I wondered whether I was right to do this work or not, whether a soldier should wear civilian clothes, whether we were not stabbing the lawful government of Vichy in the back, whether we were not playing only the part of common criminals and enemy agents for which we English in 1940 had so reviled the Germans, whether we were not employing the dirty tricks of thugs and gangsters like a treacherous Fifth Column. For we were attacked by the quisling government as Communist terrorists and murderers, and when caught faced only the public shame of prison and execution. Therein lay the real value of my D.S.O. and why I finally decided to accept it.

And the particular type of operation which I specialized in was on a larger scale than anything tried previously. Where two men had been usually sent before, I took seven and ten. We had no inside help from Frenchmen and worked completely alone. Once I was told officially that the work could not be done in that way and when we left the first time, Colonel S[†] said it would be a miracle if we succeeded, and I was only wasting lives. The Americans to begin with approved of the work of agents but not ours. We were regarded as an experiment, and when we failed the first time everybody said, 'I told you so'. I myself was called foolhardy for going into France at all with my English accent and looking such a complete Englishman (I was nearly turned down as useless by the organization for this reason when I volunteered at the very beginning); and when finally I took among the others two men, who neither

[†] Lieutenant Colonel George Starr

spoke nor understood a word of French, it was regarded as reckless and laughable in the extreme.

Then also there was the cause of democracy. I felt it was important to show too that our class too did not lack the necessary courage and endurance, though as a result I found myself alone among a band of rather desperate men, Foreign Legionaries, Communists and the like. Several had fought in the Spanish civil war, some had already been condemned to death by the Germans in North Africa. It seemed often strange company for the Brigade of Guards, and yet I was certain that real courage was beyond nationality and class, just as in France to-day Jews and Communists and priests and aristocrats all fight together in the underground war. For I feel that more than ever our class to-day is on trial before the world.

And finally in my own life — should I die this spring on the battlefields of Europe, I die as a volunteer for this special and hazardous work in a cause that I believe in with ever-increasing certainty. For the ideas of Nazi philosophy are infinitely more far-reaching than those of the French Revolution, and more diabolic than anything yet known in the history of the West. The Nazis to-day are not just the enemies of my State as the French at Waterloo or the Germans in 1914, but they are the destroyers of everything European and Christian and embody the very forces of evil. God knows we in this country are far from perfect, but this war is far more of a Crusade than the Crusades themselves ever were, did men but see the issues clearly beneath all the false flattery and clichés of the Press. We fight to-day not against ignorant heathens, or Vandals who know not the value of what they destroy, but against conscious and calculating anarchists, who strike at national culture and religion, precisely because they know that cathedrals and schools are the nerve centres of that spirit which they aim completely and for ever to destroy. The men who resist this revolution in Europe now with their lives are martyrs to a very real extent. But this side of the wall no one understands that.

And, if I survive, I shall again have passed under the shadow of the sword, and I do not believe that any man's life would be so spared unless God intended it for some special purpose. And I think that by that time that purpose will be made manifest to me. Perhaps I shall be called to the renunciation of the world, to which I have already arrived by reason and negative attraction, though for the final decision one needs the shock of something from outside and the call of God — as Ignatius Loyola was wounded and Saint Paul blinded and Saint Teresa of Avila smitten by suffering and illness. For, like the truth, that vision lies at the bottom of a deep pool, and it needs the impact of a stone to stir the waters and allow one to see through to that underlying reality, which, once comprehended, no man could ever turn away from again, though that way lies only poverty and loneliness and the Cross.

I go north in a few days' time to prepare for the final and most dangerous part of my mission. If I die, I die happy serving God's will — and if I live, perhaps it will be also in some inscrutable fashion according to that will. Either way I am at peace and content.

January 1944

Since writing this last page, acting on a strange and sudden impulse, I changed my mind completely and am returning to my regiment. I said goodbye to my colonel this morning and walked out of that room for the last time, with the map of France spread across one wall. His parting words as we shook hands were 'God bless you'— and so ended another chapter in my life.

I am going back into the Army because that is a far harder medium for idealism. Now I will work towards the same end through the technique of tanks and the barrack square rather than parachutes and explosives. If I and Julian can bring a spark into men's lives before they die my own life will have been worth while.

'*Ciò che Dio vuole io voglio.*' (The motto in Italian of the Dormer family meaning 'What God wills, I will.')

BEFORE THE INVASION

February 1944

Last night I drove into York with Julian and we dined together at the Station Hotel for the last time, before he left the battalion for good to return to Lingfield. He had been in the battalion continuously for four years, and had fought with it at Boulogne and the Hook of Holland, and it must have gone hard to leave it now on the eve of the great campaigns.

Who could have foreseen a year ago when I left Warminster that our two roles would tonight be so completely reversed? Who could have foreseen then that I would ever return to the old order against which I had seemed to set my face forever, and now a year later be bidding farewell to Julian? Both times as I climbed up into the fuselage of the Halifax the 2nd Battalion could not have seemed more remote — and yet often the way to find things in life is to turn your back on them and walk away.

And to-night as I walked across to the Mess under the full moon my thoughts could not help but go back to our friends in France, and to the men and women who would be out and working in those silent fields at this same hour. And yet far from feeling a shirker and ashamed I know that this is how they would like to see me best, in the uniform of an Irish Guardsman soon to return and liberate them.

And now having once passed through the valley of death I know well the ordeal we shall soon be facing across those seas in the spring. When one is young and inexperienced, the first clash is all excitement and adventure, but now I am more tired than I realize or would like to admit. The first bloom of youth is gone, it is now only the hard path of duty. Julian agreed over the dinner table, and told me how, when he drove down the second time to Dover to leave for Boulogne a week after the Hook of Holland, he felt very heavy and sad, while the guardsman driving beside him, who had never yet known action or seen men die, laughed and sang all the way.

After I had bid good-bye to Julian I drove back to Duncombe Park with Butler, one of the nicest Irish lads in the battalion. We talked of war, and he said he was sure he would not be killed, as he was not good enough to die, and only the best were taken.

(Wednesday) February 9th

Today the Guards Division was inspected by General Montgomery in an enormous hangar on Driffield Aerodrome. He looked tired and old as he walked between the ranks of silent, curious guardsmen. He had the bloodshot staring eyes of a fanatic and God knows into what ruthless adventures we shall be led. I felt that the sight of that great concourse, representing the *élite* of the invasion army, trained for that role over the last four years, would have gladdened the eyes of M.D. in Lyons or my hosts in Paris. It was a fitting irony that I should have escaped from the bloodhounds that morning on the hillside to return into this atmosphere and these high and ancient traditions.

(Thursday) February 24th

We drove out a fortnight ago on the Corps Exercise, which I should think will be our last exercise in England before the invasion of Europe. As the long line of Sherman tanks moved down the road from Duncombe Park and passed the ruins of Helmsley Castle in the February sunlight, I wondered what the ghosts of those Norman warriors must have thought to see this body of soldiers so soon to set out from their native country once again on the greatest of all invasions.

The next fortnight with its cold and rain and the hard nights was the most enjoyable of my Army career. To feel oneself back again among one's own countrymen — and to hear the old familiar swearwords and the native humour — to experience again the comradeship of guardsmen — all this was doubly sweet after the months I had passed without it. You have to leave your own country to appreciate it, and the instinctive goodness and fellowship of our people.

Though now and again my mind would slip back into the strange world of my memories, and I would wake at morning in the darkness of a tank bivouac and imagine myself back in France again and lost with amazement to find myself in such surroundings and beside the dark forms who snored and murmured in their sleep under the blankets. Living side by side with four men in the narrowness of a bivouac for fourteen days, you soon see the nature of men, and I am always amazed at the patience and comradeship and consideration of guardsmen. To return again at the end to the aloof discipline of the barrack square seems an awful anticlimax, and I should imagine that those sublime moments of sacrifice on a battlefield must bind men together into eternity.

One afternoon General Adair, commanding the Guards Division, came round and inspected the battalion, and I was introduced to him, and he shook me by the hand and congratulated me on my decoration.

Most evenings Fr. Curran would say Mass for the tank crews, and the setting was very peaceful and romantic. Once it was held in a cowshed at Keasey Farm while darkness fell outside the shuttered windows and there echoed in the tramp of soldiers and the crackle of a wireless set, while inside in the quiet darkness the guardsmen knelt on the straw. The white-washed walls and the thatched roofs reminded me strongly of Ireland. Snow was falling as we walked back to our squadron afterwards.

Another evening Mass was said behind a haystack in an open field. All around against the hedges the tanks were camouflaged, pointing in their silence so perfectly the contrast of peace and war. As night fell fires were lit along the lines, serving as a background to the supreme sacrifice that was being celebrated in the corner of the field. As I gazed at the shadows thrown by the Crucifix on the table I wondered how many of these men here would have paid the price of war before six months had passed. But there are worse things than death, would men only realize it; and if

ever a man, faced with the bitter and deliberate alternatives, chooses safety above honour, he will regret that
decision to his dying day and be powerless to make it again.
He who would save his life must lose it. That I think is one
of the great truths of the world, but so many men have to
make the wrong decision before they understand that there
is a certain price at which it is useless to save one's life.

The last morning I drove my tank home to Duncombe
Park in high spirits and only full of regret that the fortnight
was over.

(Friday) March 17th. St. Patrick's Day

Once again all these strange months I heard the drums
and fifes playing reveille as they marched through the
camp. It was a fine sunny morning and men were sweeping
the road in shirtsleeves — almost like summer. At nine
o'clock the Roman Catholics drove over to Ampleforth for
High Mass. It seemed incongruous to see the guardsmen
standing in the same pews where I used to pray as a boy in
the school, and monks remarked to me afterwards that the
smell of khaki was very noticeable in the Abbey Church.
The slow plaintive melody of the Benedictine plain chant
rose and fell like the sea calling men out of the world, as
perhaps many of the guardsmen there soon would be called.
The whole scene burned itself into my memory, and it
would be strange to look back upon in the years ahead.

Afterwards at eleven o'clock there was the parade for the
presentation of the shamrock on the grass in Duncombe
Park. The battalion looked very smart drawn up in the sunlight. Field Marshall Lord Cavan came on parade to present
the shamrock and afterwards we marched past on the road.

In the afternoon I bicycled over to Hawnby for tea — a
peaceful little village tucked away in the hills, which could
not have been remoter from the war.

After dinner I left the others rowdy-making and walked
down the hill past Helmsley Castle under the stars. Once
again, as when I leant over the bridge at Oxford exactly a
year ago, I knew that the future stretched away in front of

me unknown — and perhaps the better for being so. Where would the next St.Patrick's Day find me? Overhead search-lights wavered, and bombers droned above me in the dark as I walked back through the lines of tanks sheeted up under the tarpaulins like rows of silent spectators.

(Monday) March 20th

After dinner — in the real eighteenth-century manner with good wine and port — we drove over to Malton to the St. Patrick's Day dance. It was the first one that I had been to since my return and I remembered only too clearly the strange and sordid circumstances of the last St. Patrick's Day which I had spent away from the regiment. The scene inside was very gay with the band playing and the lights and couples sliding past on the floor. It all seemed now very right and proper to see such carefree festivity like the great ball at Brussels before Waterloo.

(Tuesday) March 21st

This afternoon the King drove round the camp and inspected his division. He looked cold and tired in the grey afternoon and I should think the experience to a man of his responsibilities must have been very harrowing. How many of this great company will be alive by the coming of autumn?

March

I went for a walk at evening down the valley to Rievaulx and let my mind drift with its memories. I realize that I could never sit back and rest till France is liberated, so urgent are the ties that bind me there. I remember the sun setting behind the hills at Lyons as I crossed the bridge over the river on my way to the station out of France; that room in the inn at Paris with its coloured curtains overlooking the cobbled street; how the woods looked in the moonlight above Barnay; the night that D and I slept in the four-poster bed at the farm, and how the boys talked and laughed with us all morning, and the last good-bye; that evening alone in the woods when we first heard the baying of the bloodhounds; the night we crossed the Pyrenees in thunder and lightning, and the exhaustion of the women; the familiar slowing down of the Halifax engines, the ground passing beneath in the moonlight, the light flashing to red and the roaring wind as one dropped out through the hole.

(Friday) March 24th

I arrived back in the Mess from Midhope to find that all was bustle and packing. On Monday the battalion was leaving Duncombe Park for good and moving out onto the Wolds. That evening dinner was rather a silent meal; for the first time the officers realized that we were on the move at last after those long four years and that the ordeal of fire really did lie ahead for each man sitting at table.

I went out to the Wolds for the next three days to help get ready the new camp. This was the greatest fun; we all worked together from morning to night putting up the tents under cloudless sunny skies. Everyone was in shirt sleeves and it was just like summer. All the men seemed in great spirits, hammering in the tent pegs, singing Irish songs. It was a relief to have left the dark, depressing trees of Duncombe Park and to be free as the skies above.

(Thursday) March 30th

The Division was inspected in a field by Winston Churchill.

(Easter Monday) April 10th

I have just completed twelve days in Scotland at a Combined Operations Camp waterproofing tanks and am now in the Lake District to fire our new secret guns. Here in Westmoreland vales the birds sing in the hedgerows and all is peace.

(Saturday) April 22nd

Today I moved down in advance to arrange for the concentration of the battalion at Brighton, and tonight, face to face again with the French coast, I realize what the future really holds, despite the tranquillity and peace of those Yorkshire valleys. And tonight, as each time before on the eve of my journeys, I find I experience that same feeling of goodness and exhilaration to know that the die is cast, and cast irrevocably, and that in a few weeks I shall once more be facing danger and death.

But this time, with Irish guardsmen to lead, who know and respect and have an affection for me — such as only Irishmen can have — my cup of happiness is full to the brim. Before I always felt the lack of men to look after and protect, being far more attracted by nature to the saving than the taking of lives, and I had been burdened with the responsibility of great projects rather than of human beings. And having a natural sympathy and love for all humanity, I know this to be my real vocation. For guardsmen and officers are all human beings and all equal under God, and each one of them, however brutish and coarse his exterior, embodies that same spark of the divine which is in all of us, and, if only given the right lead and inspiration, it can be fanned until it burns like a fire. I am certain from my own experience that, if you appeal sincerely and fearlessly to the best side of men, they will nearly always respond and prefer such an appeal to one which merely seeks to talk down to them in their own coarse language. Certain people like Julian Stonor are intended as beacons to the world, reminding men of the eternal existence of those high ideals which call men out against all reason and self-interest; and if there came a time when the race of such sentinels as he had died out or were fallen asleep, then humanity would sink into perpetual despair, seeing only its daily round of sordid suffering and dull monotony. And I, as a poet, know that there is more idealism about soldiers than about anybody else, for on a battlefield one witnesses the phenomenon of the ordinary citizen raised up to the heights of sublime heroism and self-sacrifice. And many of my fellow officers, who hitherto have seen only the different tastes and the brutish side of guardsmen, are appreciating for the first time that they are human beings exactly like themselves, and their letters. when they read and censor them, inspire them deeply with the guardsmen's sincerity and loving devotion to their wives. Our class has sometimes learnt to be elegant at the sacrifice of the natural virtues, and guardsmen are rarely other than simple like children, and that is a quality which I prize and envy above all others.

Yet also I am a practical man as well as a dreamer of humanity and, just because one looks for the souls of men, it does not mean that one is blind to the blemishes of their bodies. Living exclusively in the society of their fellow men and cut off for long periods from the refining influence of women and their homes, guardsmen tend to develop a shell of hardness and coarseness and cynicism. It is difficult to remain gentle and not to be hardened if you have to lead a hard life. On the road down to Brighton we passed in the Jeep the scene of an accident and there was a man groaning on the side with blood pouring from his temples and one leg crumpled up, and it gave one a little idea of what a battlefield must look like, and the hallowed beaches where English blood will flow. There can be very little idealism about war at the time, but only a lot of dirt and fear and sickening ignominy. It is only in retrospect or in the roman-tic minds of those who have never witnessed the horrors of a battlefield that glory is seen.

And yet after my experience I know, what I originally sur-mised, that the only happy man is he who serves some ideal other than his own self-interest. All ambitious men who have purely personal objectives will never be satisfied but will only realize each day more and more the futility and worthlessness of their ambitions. While in contrast, the man who seeks sacrifice and service each day feels more deeply within his soul that glow of true happiness. There is so much in the world to appreciate and so much goodness in each individual human being to love that it would take an eterni-ty to complete, and yet at the end of it all to die for God and one's country and one's fellow men would be the greatest blessing of all. Those who fall in battle, and are thereby privileged with the opportunity to make that supreme act of self-sacrifice, are the truly fortunate and those who return to the humdrum world have the hardest part to bear.

And here in England, as you walk along the green hedgerows under the budding trees and watch the shimmer of the heat haze on the sea, you can feel the sap rising in the young veins of our soldiers. And as I watch this great company of men assembling around me in these the closing days of our preparations, I am weighed down by the same feeling of sadness as I felt at the end of my last term before leaving school. For the last time the gathering is complete before it breaks up; afterwards the moment is unique and irrevocable, and to-morrow the actors will all be scattered to the ends of the earth. And watching the soldiers working on their trucks and armoured cars, I see that I never realized before how much I love my own people with all their faults and all their shortcomings. For they are my people and I would gladly die for them.

April

On my way down through London I called in at the War Office to see my former head. He told me that D was probably dead and there was little news of the others. Life was becoming increasingly dangerous with the constant mass arrests and executions. When would the Army strike? I climbed back into my Jeep and continued on my way to Brighton.

Down here it is early summer with the song of birds and green trees and a shimmer on the sea. In Parliament Ernest Bevin spoke of the silence that lay over all the land.

(Friday) May 5th

Last night I dreamt that I revisited again the Pyrenees and passed once more by a prison in Spain. And going in I found D lying in bed in the darkness, and when he heard my voice he wept silently. The gaoler told me that he was still alive but sorrowful to death.

(Friday) May 12th

Julian Stonor came down to Brighton to-day and in the evening we walked out to the Devil's Dyke and sat there for a long time as the light failed, looking out over the vale of the Sussex hills. We talked of the unique mellowness and richness of the English countryside, of how the whole art and achievement of life was to learn how to appreciate the myriad beauty of humanity and the universe as the creation of God, and then to educate one's people in the same technique. Men must be reminded of the extraordinary nature of the everyday world, of the wonders and the beauty of the spirit, or else they become drowned in the slough of despond and overcome by the drabness and sordidness of their all-encompassing life. The man who lives in a slum beside a London railway line must surely despair, if he really believes that his drab world of shadows is indeed the only one. We agreed that for those who had been given the imagination and the power, their mission was to appeal to the higher side of human nature and to remind men of the eternal values, rather than to plunge into the fellowship of the common level. As Chesterton saw, there was a fairy world in everything if you could only see it — a deeper sense of appreciation. Why should men walk through life blind and dumb?

We walked back under the evening star with a young Sussex farmer whom we met out rabbit shooting.

May

Julian came down again and we dined together on the Front and sat on a bench by the sea. We talked of the philosophy of danger, and of how incredible it was that the majority of men shrank from the prospect of the Second Front and wanted only to return to the mantelpiece of their fireside. Surely, given the opportunity, men would prefer to do something fine in their life once, even if the price was death? What attraction had the humdrum world of their ordinary lives compared with the heroism and sacrifices of the battlefield?

(Monday) May 15th

Prince John of Luxembourg came over to dinner with me and we talked of pine forests and America, of Europe and the English character, of broadmindedness and patriotism, of Catholicism and Ampleforth. Alec Creighton was there too and we talked at length of 'The Years of Endurance'.

(Wednesday) May 17th

Tonight the sky has been filled with the roar of bombers passing out across the Channel and the whole tempo of life has so been stepped up that the date of the invasion is obviously at hand. The tanks are all stowed with ammunition and are merely waiting for the word.

Once again I face the unknown, though this time there is a deadly earnestness about it all which makes the experience of my journeys before seem like child's play in comparison; and also I feel that this time the die is certain and the path of duty leads one way irrevocably. This time there will be no coming back; I feel it in my bones, and in this knowledge I set out. My life has built up to this climax and there are moments when I wonder whether I have not already left this world. I feel I belong so utterly and completely to the men of this battalion that if one is wounded, I am wounded, and if one dies, I die.

Last night I talked to my troop about the journey which we would soon be making, and I told them how they were first and foremost soldiers and everything else was only leisure and recreation, and that the time was approaching when they would have to show whether they were really guardsmen or no — and as I talked in the failing light of the room their faces seemed to glow up at me out of the darkness with a very deep earnestness.

There is a noticeable air of contentment and relief about the battalion this last week, for everybody feels that the die is cast now once and for all, finally and irrevocably. I read today of the capture of Cassino by General Juin's troops, and I can very easily imagine the sensations of the conquerors. On a battlefield the great truths are learnt in all their horrible simplicity and greater love than this no man hath...

Meanwhile all is still here and the birds sing in the trees and there are flowers on Our Lady's altar in the church. Julian Stonor has apparently left us for good, and I feel that his responsibilities have somehow fallen on me too.

I am deeply happy and feel that somehow I have reached the summit and the end. *Ciò che Dio vuole io voglio.*

Shortly before the Invasion

Before the time comes for me to set out across the Channel for the third time, I have decided to set out the reasons why I threw over my former employment and, just at the very moment of its final glory and fruition, changed back once again into the uniform of an Irish Guardsman.

When I intended to leave and was offered another and immediate job it was this. I should have been dropped by parachute on the February moon to a reception committee, who would have put me in touch with the different groups of Frenchmen hiding in the Maquis of the West. I would have travelled among them all over France, advising and training them for their role in the invasion, employing my own military knowledge. Certain plateaux would have to be reconnoitred for the eventual landing of the Airborne Division, and their defence organized. Arms and ammunition would be stored and I would be the Inspector-General of the different patriot bands. The value of my reconnaissance would lie in my returning to England before the planning of the invasion, and I would be taken in March to a certain area in the north of France where I would be picked up by Lysander aircraft. As my accent was so poor I would have to live hidden all this time in the mountains. Before leaving I would have to have gone to Algiers to see de Gaulle.

But when the time comes to fight in the open for the liberation of France in a few weeks, then it must be a Frenchman who will lead the French, and a man too who has stayed in his own country and shared the sufferings of the dark hours, not one dropped form the skies at the last moment, a foreigner and unproved. The French are not analogous to the ignorant tribes of Abyssinia — they need no foreign leaders like Wingate to command their guerrilla forces.

Similarly and by the same argument at the approaching climax of the war, my duty will be towards my own people

as a soldier and an officer. I had originally taken up this
work as the only activity open to me during those long
months when my Division together with the armies of Liberation trained and assembled on the peaceful hills of
England. And I had always known and hoped at the back of
my mind, when I left them, that I would return to the Irish
Guards when the time for soldering at last arrived. For that
reason I had avoided any further promotion that might
make my return impossible. I had refused the extra pay of
my captaincy knowing that, if I returned, it would be to my
old rank of subaltern. I had kept the Guards Armoured
Divisional sign on one suit of battledress that hung always
in my wardrobe at Cranmer Court. And I had felt always at
the back of my mind that somehow, sometime, in the end, I
would return to fight in the 2nd Battalion.

I am sure too that regimental soldiering with all the hard
duty and physical horror of a battlefield is a far higher and
more arduous life than one of irresponsible adventure. A lot
of my former companions, I felt, possessed no loyalties anywhere, and some had already played the same game in
South America and the Foreign Legion and Spain. And
that is a very selfish life in itself and appeals more to hatred
of the enemy than love of one's country. An organization
that sets out to organize and harness that hatred to its own
political ends treads a morally dangerous path. Guerrilla
fighting often breeds a race of professionally mercenary soldiers who love war and can only live in a violent, restless
and destructive atmosphere. And another of my reasons for
returning to my regiment had been the fear of being asked
to do things that I did not agree with. To lead armed bands
of hungry, desperate men behind the enemy lines at the
invasion, each individual eager for revenge against his own
political enemies and obviously beyond my control and
restraint, was a nightmare that had often haunted my
future. Hitherto I had undertaken precise and definite roles
with which I was in complete agreement — but to take on a
general mission of indefinite scope would be a very different

matter; one's initiative can lead one sometimes into some very strange decisions, following the insidious principle of total warfare and the ends that justify the means. I had already been acquainted with the assassin of Darlan and knew of the existence of similar briefings. There was also the woman who got herself injected with V.D., and then returned to France to sleep with as many German soldiers as she could. I have never spilt human blood yet and, if I must, then I will do it impersonally and in obedience to orders, and not in cold murder or as the tool of London. Death now seemed inevitable and I preferred to meet it in uniform.

And this too is what I am sure the people of France would like me to do, to prove to them that I was a soldier and to return in uniform and liberate them. They always liked to think that they were helping and sheltering officers and not spies. And also during this last year I had repeatedly received letters from guardsmen asking me to return, and I had promised Brown in the Orderly Room before my last journey that, if I returned from it, I would come back to the battalion, and I knew that in a way when the hour of action struck they relied on me to see them through it. When the time comes to fight a battalion does need inspiration and men whom it knows and trusts; and the human beings who compose it with all their weakness and failings need resolute leadership — and I have often thought that the officers are sometimes not good enough for the men. Of one thing I am sure, that extremely dark hours lie ahead of the battalion that will test men to the uttermost.

And so for all these reasons and more I had turned down that offer of a really extraordinary job with its fame and scope for ambition. I remembered in the *Seven Pillars of Wisdom* Lawrence's advice to posterity: 'I pray God that no other English lad reading this story will from love of the glamour of strangeness go out to prostitute himself and his talents in the service of another race.' It is a far higher ideal to lead an ordinary life in an extraordinary manner, and to serve an ideal amid the drab and humdrum surroundings of everyday life and to retain that vision of the common man as the shadow of God. I am certain that it will be far harder to face the bullets than the Gestapo.

While I was deciding which path to follow at this — perhaps the most important cross road of my career — I passed through a dark night of the soul with sleepless nights and terrific uncertainty, being pulled both ways at once. I took my problem to Our Lady and the Little Flower and asked them to decide.

I walked to the War Office that morning and locked myself again within the gates of the prison of the army. I told them that in the end I had decided that I was a guardsman. Pray God that it was the right decision and that He will give me the courage to go through with it to the end.

(Thursday) May 25th

We were inspected on the sea front by General Eisenhower. He walked down the ranks.

Paddy Pole Carew fell ill suddenly and was taken to hospital. In the general shuffle round I was made a captain again. The wheel has come full circle[1].

I am sending this book away to-morrow, as I think the hour will strike in the next few days and my final journey will have begun. God knows no man ever set out more happily or gladly before — and lead where it may, I follow the path in ever-mounting spirits. God grant me the courage not to let my guardsmen down, knowing as I do how they count on me. I ask only that He do with my life as He wills — if I should be privileged to give it on the field of battle, then indeed would the cup be full. There are times when I feel the tide of happiness so mounting in my soul as though the flood-gates might burst and the frail body and its bonds break asunder. My soul is exhilarated like a bird that would sing for ever till its lungs burst.

No man ever went out to meet his fate more joyfully than I.

[1] In order to rejoin his regiment Hugh Dormer had to lose his S.O.E Captain's rank and return to his rank of subaltern.

CHAPTER FIVE

THE 2ND BATTALION IN FRANCE

July

At eight a.m. on June 6th, 1944, it was announced on the wireless that at dawn that morning the Royal Navy had begun disembarking the Allied Armies on the northern coasts of France. At that moment all doubts and apprehensions had been set at rest; it was no longer a matter of discussing the possibility of the operation; the enterprise had finally, after four years of speculation, been embarked upon.

The news was received on the tank park with tremendous excitement. Guardsmen were asked into nearby houses to listen to the wireless; women stopped me in the street to shake hands and wish me and my men all luck and a safe return. However cynical the soldiers might be, the people of England, whom they were going out to represent, seemed fully conscious of their crusading mission. To myself personally the news was an enormous relief, to know finally that I was on the road back and that my promises, made in quiet rooms in Lyons and Paris, in farms in Autun and the Pyrenees, were now to be realized.

Three days before on the way back from the ranges I and Peter Agnew had passed a column of tanks and trucks moving down to Newhaven. The men in the vehicles neither grinned nor catcalled to the passers-by as usual but stared out with a certain silent solemnity. I had seen that look before and knew from the expression on their faces that this was no exercise but the real thing.

A week later[†] we received the order to move and early the next morning the battalion moved out from Brighton to the marshalling area. The rumble of the tanks broke the Sunday morning sleepiness of the town; as we passed the Pavilion with its atmosphere of the Regency bucks, it

[†] Sunday, June 11th

seemed a very suitable setting-out point for the Guards Division. All that day we drove across typical English countryside with thatched cottages and honeysuckle in the hedgerows and the cornfields gleaming in the June heat. I gazed at the passing panorama and feasted my eyes on its peculiar fragrance and richness; alone in Europe, England had known always the blessing of liberty and peace, and remembering the experiences of my former travels I stored up those sun-drenched memories that morning against the bleak and terrible future. To one locked in the prison, those springs of life alone make life bearable. Edward Grey garnered up enough happiness in five years of married life to last twenty years of solitary blind old age. Through many long nights of walking in the mountains of Spain the mind had slipped back unconsciously into scenes at Ampleforth and Oxford, of cricket matches in the summer term and life with the Irish Guards.

We arrived in the marshalling area at six p.m. and worked till midnight under the full moon, completing the final stages of water-proofing.

The next fortnight passed in rather dreary waiting. The storm had smashed most of the landing craft on the French coast. One afternoon I went down to Portsmouth and went over the *Victory*. Standing beneath the low, shady beams of the cabin in the cockpit of the ship where Nelson died it was easy to recapture the atmosphere of the scene. I am sure that at the time it was all perfectly ordinary; a battle was raging above deck like any other battle; the admiral was dying as millions of other men have died in battle. Only posterity has seen the significance of the scene in perspective and created the legend; so that years later the oaks in Chesterton's garden were always to remind him of the timbers of that cabin.

At last once again we received the order to move, and the tanks drove down to embark at Portsmouth. This again seemed very appropriate, seeing that it was from Portsmouth that I first sailed in the destroyer two years ago and got that sight of the French coast lit by bursting star shells in the night action that started me on my travels.

We loaded the tanks on to the landing craft and then moved out to take up our station in the convoy. The sight of that mass of shipping in the roads with the battleships of the fleet anchored at their moorings was extraordinary indeed. As far as the eye could see stretched ships and ships and ships. The dream of Dunkirk had indeed come true.

Towards seven the convoy moved out and, watching the Hampshire shores receding in the failing light, it was like lying in the fuselage of a Halifax bomber flying out over German-occupied France. My third travel was beginning at this time; though less spectacular than before, it would be the hardest and the longest of the three. I did not share the light-hearted optimism of my companions and knew very well what bitter fighting lay ahead. Once more I could not see the end of the journey nor where this adventure was leading. Of the laughing group in the ship setting out that evening how many would return, and how many like their fathers before them, would lie for ever in France?

I stood in the bow of the ship talking to the men till night fell. We rolled in the sea and the spray came stinging over the sides. Once again I had to rub my eyes to see the tanks and guardsmen on the ships at last. This night was the climax of the weary years of training in the desolate places of England, the sight which men had talked and dreamed about but never really thought would come. I was far too excited for sleep, but sat up in my blankets all night as we cut through the waves. Once more life had a purpose and once again one was really living.

Soon after daylight the morning sun shone on the cliffs of France. Beneath them lay anchored in the roads the mightiest concentration of ships ever seen in the Channel. Battleships and cruisers rocked on the swell. With field-glasses one could pick out the ruined outline and staring windows of the houses on the edge. Wrecked tanks and landing craft were stranded on the beach and behind them

in the fields poppies stood out in great patches of red. With
the parallel of Flanders, the poppies seemed a very appropriate sight to greet the eyes of the next generation.

That night we drove into the harbour area, where the
battalion lay up round a corn field for the next two weeks.
This was a real gipsy life that suited me down to the ground,
and to have the opportunity of being both a guardsman and
a gipsy was surely an ideal and rare combination. It was a
splendid life to sleep out in the open under the sky and to
be woken by the chill of the dawn and the cooing of pigeons
in the trees above, as years ago in my childhood they used to
coo under my window in Kenya; to have breakfast cooked
by oneself round a wood fire and then to get everything
cleared up for parade. The day would pass putting the finishing touches to the tanks and getting then ready for action.
Sometimes there would be an early morning run through
the rose-covered villages or a visit to the first battlefields,
where on either side of a road only a few hundred yards
apart lay the shattered burnt-out wrecks of Panther and
Sherman tanks. In the afternoon we would take the men
bathing in a nearby river and afterwards I would walk down
into St. Martin les Entrées to hear Mass in the village
church. The guardsmen would line the side of the field and
watch the ceaseless stream of ambulances, tanks and trucks
pouring up to the front line. At evening I would walk round
the bivouacs, talking to the crews round the smouldering
fires as it grew dark, while the thudding of the guns at Caen
shook the quiet peace of our cornfield. And then back to my
own tank to sit round with the four other guardsmen of my
crew talking of all things of heaven and earth. Over all our
heads, consciously or unconsciously, hung the Damoclean
sword of the approaching battle and I, who knew the Germans and the land, told them that it would be a fight to the
death and the road to victory would be bloody and long.
And so to bed with the thudding of the distant guns. Thus
passed the last days of the ordinary soldiers who waited
before the Waterloo of the twentieth century.

One evening I walked down after dinner to a nearby farm and talked with a man there who had come through the German lines at night from Caen. He had three children and the youngest had been killed by shellfire and his wife wounded in the face. His home had been occupied by troops of an S.S. Panzer Division, who had shot five Canadian prisoners before his eyes. Talking of those terrible things in that quiet field seemed some strange fantasy. On the way back, I watched the R.A.F. putting in their big attack on Caen which was to be the prelude to the great assault. For an hour the Lancasters circled and dived down over the German lines in the teeth of fierce anti-aircraft fire. One could see the shells and the tracer bursting in the sky, and once a German plane flew low enough overhead for one to see the face of one's enemy. I was reminded of the death of Michael Marks and the sensation of being hated personally, which I had always before found so hard to understand and experience. I returned to the squadron as though to another world of the drinking and laughter of unblooded troops. Soon they too would pass through the valley of death.

Another evening we took the men for an early run and passed by six English graves on the roadside. They were covered with roses and lilies by the French farmer who owned the field, and each one had at its head a clean white cross. 'The sword also means cleanness and death.'

To-day I got a letter from Italy from B which took me back into those days and nights hiding in the French woods behind German lines. I looked to-day at the map of patriot activities in France and imagined myself too again in those hills and I remembered the baying of the bloodhounds.

On Sunday† the battalion went to Mass in the Cathedral at Bayeux. And it stirred me, as it always does, to see the tall neat figures of the guardsmen before the altar and their contrast with the lawless fanatics of my former revolutionary days. To my mind they have always represented

† July 16th

the ideal combination — 'Guardsmen in peace and devils in war'.

Today was O'Connor's twenty-first birthday. He is my operator and as good-natured and religious a young man as you would ever meet anywhere. Every night I used to see him at Mass in the village church and he was always only too eager to help me without ever even asking. He made my bed up at night and cleaned my belt and shoes and looked after me always. He was at a Jesuit school when the war broke out and, like many guardsmen, had a very real idea of what fighting honourably means. He agreed with me when I deplored the scanty treatment of German graves in comparison to our own. Both sides, though enemies, had fought as brave men and deserved equal honours of war.

A local farmer had given him a bouquet of roses for his birthday and four eggs, for he had Irish blood in his veins and a way with him. So the crew had a great breakfast with the flowers on the packing-case table in the open between the tanks. When we leave next week for the greatest battle of the world, I am taking the flowers with me in the turret as a memory and a fragrance of nicer things in all that unpleasantness. The scent of roses might help to perfume a little the smell of cordite and burning flesh.

Tonight we received the first orders of the great battle of France, the climax of the whole four years of war and the second front. Listening to the sober prosaic details of the military machine I knew once again that the die was cast and that the path of honour led one way and one way alone and irrevocably. And I am exhilarated and on fire again.

To-morrow we set out on what, I suppose, we hope will bring about the final decision of the war. The plan is bold and on a grand scale and many men will lose their lives in the accomplishment of it. The R.A.F. in their bombardment are sure to cause the most terrible destruction of the whole war on the French villages. Then men, who lie about sleeping on the grass this afternoon and who have never yet seen

¹ Tuesday, July 18th

action, will to-morrow witness the most horrible sights of fire and death that have ever been seen before in Europe.

I face the adventure in sober determination, knowing how I shall feel and knowing that modern armoured war is Hell, and complete Hell, and nothing else, with no nobility or fineness about it, but only humiliating fear. Once again at Mass this morning I offered my life to God to do with it entirely as He chooses. Should He take it, then indeed would I be happy and go forth eagerly to meet that death, having only sorrow for my mother left behind. But then all men must die sometime, and for a long time I have felt a stranger on this earth. *Ciò che Dio vuole io voglio.*

EPILOGUE

The 2nd Armoured Battalion Irish Guards, as part of the Guards Armoured Division, fought its first battle on July 18th in the great armoured attack east of Caen. After four days the Division was withdrawn, granted a rest and then on July 29th moved to Caumont on the right of the British sector to carry out another attack southwards through a gap made by the 15th (S) Division.

The battalion drove most of the next day and night, and then joined up with an infantry battalion, 5th Battalion Coldstream Guards, to make a battle group On the afternoon of July 31st it was ordered to advance to capture some high ground near the little village, St. Martin des Besaces, some six miles south of Caumont. The country was typical Bocage, thick woods, high hedges and sunken lanes. The 2nd Armoured Battalion Irish Guards started from well behind the front, and the roads were blocked with the transport of three Divisions.

The plan was that Hugh Dormer's squadron, No. 2, which was part of Squadron H.Q., should support the infantry attack on the high ground. The attack began in the dusk down the main road. Nothing definite was known of the enemy, so targets were mostly speculative. Only a few German L.M.G.s replied. By nightfall part of the objective had been gained and the infantry dug in, and the tanks came back to harbour behind them. Because of the terrain it was impossible for a complete account of the action to be given. At the muster Hugh Dormer's tank was missed, and wireless calls to him went unanswered.

By the next afternoon the enemy had been driven back and a search of the battlefield located his tank where a fire had been seen burning the night before. Two of the crew had been killed outright, and Hugh Dormer's body lay among some German dead nearby. It appears that while ahead of the Squadron he must have sighted and attacked an enemy post. His tank was then hit by A.T.K. fire from the side, where it went on fire. Hugh Dormer was wounded. Then, trying to make his way back on foot, he was shot, and the two surviving guardsmen captured.

He was buried with the others by the roadside. At his funeral guardsmen came with bunches of flowers for his grave. A brother officer wrote in a letter home: 'they loved him because they knew he loved them. They will miss him even more than we will.' The local French farmer offered to look after the graves. He said it would be a small return for the debt that France owed to the British dead.

APPENDIX

*FOUR DAYS IN HMS ALBRIGHTON WHILE
ENGAGED ON SPECIAL OPERATIONS TO INTER-
CEPT AN ENEMY ARMED MERCHANT RAIDER IN
THE ENGLISH CHANNEL*

Sunday, October 11th, 1942

1830 hours. Moved out of Portsmouth in the October twilight in company with HMS *Gleasdale, Eskdale, Quorn,
Ferney* and *Cottismore*, forming up outside the boom in line
astern of six destroyers. Lights flash in the mist as we
receive our orders by lamp signal. Speed twenty knots.

1930 hours. The wardroom, being below decks, has closed.
Dinner is served in the Captain's cabin. A general feeling of
exhilaration and the certainty of intercepting the raider
tonight. The plan of battle is that the three " gun" Hunts
leading should engage the cruiser and her escort with fire,
while we and the other two torpedo Hunts move to a flank
and put in the attack. After dinner we snatch an hour's
sleep while the ship steams on.

2300 hours. Action stations sound as we enter the German
minefields. I throw a Duffel coat over my Mae West and
grope my way up through the wheel house on to the bridge.
It is dark and at first my eyes can see nothing. Then I pick
up the dim figures clustered in front. There must be about
twenty men on the bridge, including signallers and search-
light crews and look out men. Everything is silent except
for the hissing of the sea. The masts slowly swing against
the sky. There are drifting clouds and here and there for an
instant some stars. The luminous paint on the torpedo
sights gleams. The captain is at the wheel and with the dark
throng of cowled figures standing round him on the raised
platform, all waiting for his commands, the picture reminds
me anciently of some master and his disciples or the vault
of a Benedictine monastery.

2400 hours. We are passing now down a lane of buoys,

whose shaded lights mark the passage that the minesweepers have cleared an hour previously. At each one a motor
launch waits to guard against any interference. Asdic and
RDF are listening out. RDF reports echoes from the French
coast ten miles away. Searchlights sweep the waters from
the distant shore. I took a turn round the iron deck and
talked in whispers to some stokers, up to get a breath of air
from the boiler room.

0100 hours. Cocoa is served on the bridge, hot and sweet.

0200 hours. Suddenly the alarm goes from the destroyer in
front. All hands are ordered to first degree readiness. RDF
has reported the presence of small craft approaching.
Another minute goes by while everybody scans the sea, trying to pierce the darkness. Then a star shell goes up and
another and another, illuminating a dark shape low in the
water ahead of us. She is instantly challenged. We wait
seven seconds but no recognition signal is flashed back. Our
forward 4-inch guns open up and fire three salvoes, while
we swing around for a torpedo attack, before the craft is
identified as one of our own STBs, which has got out of
position. The firing ceases and we return home in line
astern.

Monday, October 12th

0600 hours. At first light a complete wing of three Spitfire
squadrons comes out to escort us in.

Tuesday, October 13th

0830 hours. We took on a week's rations and reverted to
immediate notice.

0930 hours. We slip again. Arrive at Dartmouth about 1500
hours. The AMC is reported by the RAF to have moved
further West and may be making a bid to complete the last
lap of her voyage to the Atlantic tonight. As we lie at our
moorings in Dartmouth harbour, evening comes down mist-
ily and gently as it always does in the West country. The
autumn woods slope down steeply to the water's edge: a
paddleboat chugs across the bay: the girls cluster outside the
Raleigh Arms not two hundred yards away, hoping for the

ship's boat to bring the Liberty men ashore. The five destroyers all lie together in the middle, causing more excitement than Dartmouth has seen since the war started. We have fuelled up and are at immediate notice. There is a captain's conference on board the *Cottismore*. The *Ferney* has gone to Plymouth to collect our force commander for the night.

1930 hours. We have a small cocktail party in the wardroom, followed by an early dinner. A singaller comes in to say that we will slip at 2030 hours. There is a launch with three Wrens alongside us below the men's quarters. But there is no laughter or catcalling as there would have been in the Army. The Devon lads are quiet and well-behaved: they have the natural cleanness and courtesy of the sea.

2030 hours. We slip out of Dartmouth in the dusk and form up in line astern outside the harbour. We have five destroyers with us, and behind us ten MTBs. That is Force A and it is our role to intercept the enemy. Force B, consisting of the other four destroyers and escorting craft are to lie off west of the Channel Islands, should the enemy give us the slip. The area is not thought to be mined so we have no sweeper in front. Our particular role in Force A is to engage the enemy with gunfire from a flank while the MTBs slip in to make the torpedo attack. As we shall not be firing torpedoes ourselves, there are no restrictions about opening fire from the forward oerlikons. As night has come down and we have three hours steaming ahead, I go below to snatch some sleep.

2330 hours. Action stations sound. On my way up to the bridge I see the 4-inch shells being hoisted up from the magazine on the mess decks.

The new moon is not yet up. Outside everything is pitch black. This time we are showing no stern lights and I can barely distinguish the faint outline of the destroyer in front. This is all we have to steer by and at times I lose sight of the *Eskdale* altogether. The captain of course has not left the wheel since leaving Dartmouth and I realize what a nerve-wracking responsibility is his. To lose your formation at sea is to run the almost certain danger of being fired on by your own side. Recognition and station-keeping in night actions is all.

The MTBs for some unaccountable reason have dropped far astern. RDF picks them up at two miles distance. They will probably miss the battle altogether and run into us on the return journey. In that case we will go in without them and make the torpedo attack ourselves. We are passing the Channel Islands now and have turned east towards Cherbourg. Lights are flashing all round us from the shore, until I am certain we have been seen and are in a trap.

2340 hours. Signal received from Plymouth giving exact bearing of the enemy convoy. We increase our speed to twenty-five knots. We should intercept them off Cap de la Hague. First degree readiness is ordered and there are constant all round sweeps on Asdic and RDF. Two small echoes are reported immediately ahead three and a half miles away. We begin to zig-jag and sharp eyes are needed at the wheel.

The gun crews are given their orders for the night and I am in charge again of the two forward oerlikons. There is an electric atmosphere on the bridge and tempers are a bit on edge. The look-outs will persist in standing in front of the torpedo sights, which may be wanted quickly. The phosphorescent wake of the destroyer in front gleams as she heels over to starboard. The night is quiet.

2400 hours. A star shell goes up in front, followed at once by a salvo from the 4-inch guns. And then Hell breaks loose, and for the next half hour there is a constant rain of star shell and tracer and salvoes.

The whole scene is brilliantly lit up. Behind, three miles away, is the French coast clearly visible. In front of it about two miles away is the German convoy. The AMC is in the middle and on either side are lanes of escorting minesweepers and E. boats and light 500-ton destroyers. Our five destroyers are steaming parallel in line astern firing broadsides as quick as the crews can load. The enemy are replying with streams of green tracer, which are poured out incessantly in long flat curves. Every ship on both sides is firing at close range and the noise is tremendous.

The 6-inch battery on the shore has opened up on us. There are white flashes ahead and spurts of water round us. A stream of red tracer passes over the mast. Our 4-inch guns have swung to 90 degrees and the blast is terrific. The cordite fumes and sparks obscure one's vision for about 8 seconds. The rear pom-pom and oerlikons are firing rhythmically, but they are out of range. The *Cottesmore* reports two torpedoes passing astern.

2400 hours. One of the R-boats has been hit and begins to glow steadily. At once every gun switches on to it and its fate is certain. The AMC has also been hit and is on fire, and two minutes later blows up with a tremendous explosion. A great cheer goes up on deck. An MTB has slipped in among our own shells and torpedoed it.

There was a tall sheet of flame and the ship literally disintegrated. I could clearly see fragments of it silhouetted against the red glow. Oil is burning on the water in an area a quarter of a mile long. The captain says that the explosion was bigger than when he had to torpedo the *Berkeley* at Dieppe. Her magazine must have exploded.

2430 hours. There is a lull in the firing. All the time the destroyers have been steaming on in line astern and the only noise now in the sudden silence is the water slipping by and the hiss of our wake.

We are turning round now and coming back down the line. There are lights flashing on three sides of us and we seem liable to run ashore at any moment. There is a thick pall of smoke and the oil is still burning furiously. There are no signs of the escort, but we are expecting an E-boat attack. Tired eyes keep seeing shapes looming up in the dark and there are frequent alarms. There are still star shells going up from the shore and the 6-inch battery has not stopped.

2440 hours. We receive the signal to disengage and to steam north at full speed.

0100 hours. As we repass the Channel Islands we see more
star shells go up and gun flashes round the head. That
must be Force B going into the attack. The C-in-C
Plymouth has signalled his congratulations to all ranks
taking part.

Tea is served on the bridge and we go to second degree
readiness. Now it is all over the Yeoman of Signals relaxes
and gives me a bar of chocolate. The star-board watch falls
out. The stars shine clearly and Orion is high up in the
southern sky. There is a fresh wind blowing. I curl up in my
Duffel coat on the oerlikon gun platform and doze off, with
the breeze and the spray stinging my face. One could lead
this life for ever. For the first time since the war started I
have known what it means to live.

Wednesday, October 14th
0750 hours. We enter wooded Dartmouth at dawn and tie
up just as people on the shore are going to their work. It is a
typical October morning, clear and cold.

PATROLLING ON AN MTB WHILE LIVING ON
BOARD THE ALBRIGHTON

Monday, November 23rd, 1942
The night before we left Yarmouth in readiness for any call
to the French coast. The night was very cold and there was
a real woodcock's moon. The ship had just returned from
North Africa the day previously, and while we swing at
anchor, I listened to the hands gossiping quietly among
themselves of Ponta and the Azores, of Flying Fortresses
landing in relays on the racecourse at Gibraltar, and of the
pineapples and Algerian wine they had brought back.
1630 hours. We left Portsmouth and formed up behind the
destroyer *Pennyland* with two MTBs following behind us.
Coastal aircraft were out ahead spotting for any movement
of enemy shipping and we were to patrol in mid Channel

waiting for their signal to cross and attack the convoy. As we passed the Flak tower at the entrance, the time honoured ritual was carried out. All guns were loaded and the pom-pom and oerlikons each fired a single round into the gathering mist. The galleys were shut down for the night. A fresh breeze was blowing and the air was brisk with the presence of the evening.

1845 hours. One MTB returned to post with electrical trouble. There were many signals flashed down the line and life on the bridge with only one signaller became rather hectic. These craft have a crew of three officers and eighteen ratings and conditions of living are very hard. Everything is cramped into minature and all the gun platforms are completely open and exposed to bullets and the wind. The bridge is small and quite unprotected. Speed is our only armour.

1900 hours. Dark fell suddenly as we were passing down the line of buoys marking the swept passage. The glow of the sunset lingered a long time over the waters.

1930 hours. We had supper on the bridge of sausages and mash and a bottle of whisky. One needed a fire within to withstand the freezing wind against one's face.

2200 hours. We reduced speed to twelve knots on reaching the patrol line. At once we started to rock in the Channel swell as the water slapped up against the side. The sea was distinctly choppy for a small craft and the other MTB returned to harbour finding it too rough. The sub-mariner, who was my fellow passenger on board, became violently sick and remained so for the rest of the night. I retired to snatch some sleep in the wardroom which, with his company, had now taken on the atmosphere of a nightmare phantasy.

0100 hours. I clutched my way up on to the bridge to find us still pitching in the swell. The moon was shining down on the waves in a bright path, toneless and unearthly as it has always appeared to me in eastern seas. One feels alone under its rays, out of time and out of the world, voyaging on for ever into limitless oceans by the light of that strange lantern.

It is only in a small ship where one is almost level with the water that I feel one with the sounding waves and their ceaseless variety and fascination. One really hears then the music of the sea, calling men out like the sirens of Charybdis to their destruction.

Jupiter was buring in the southern sky and near it that mystical pattern of Orion, whose symmetry always seems a phenomenon and sign to men. And near it again the Pleiades. The White Ensign streamed from the mast and every now and again spray came stinging over the bridge. In front stood out the silhouette of the *Pennyland* with her tall masts like some crusader's cross proudly borne ahead as though on an ancient banner. So passed the hours coldly.

0700 hours. At first light we had tea on the bridge as we headed for Portsmouth. We passed a line of minesweepers just setting out. I leant against the mast-head while the cold wind and the spray made one's eyes glow as though they held the coals of that inner and eternal fire.

0930 hours. Both watches were piped up to attention as we passed the C-in-C's flagship on our return to harbour after a sixteen hour patrol.